JET CITY REWIND

Aviation History of Seattle and the Pacific Northwest

Timothy A. Nelson

Schiffer Publishing Ltd

4880 Lower Valley Road · Atglen, PA 19310

Copyright © 2016 by Timothy A. Nelson

Library of Congress Control Number: 2016935659

Designed by Brenda McCallum

Cover image: Author's composite of two images: 2013 photo of Seattle skyline and last of the Boeing 314 Clippers, NC18612 *Cape Town Clipper*, taking off from Elliott Bay circa 1941. *Courtesy of the author and The Boeing Company Collection at The Museum of Flight.*

Title page image: *The Boeing Company Collection at The Museum of Flight.* See page 41 for caption.

Page 4 image: Boeing Field and surroundings circa 1950. The edge of Boeing Plant 2 is at lower right. New Boeing B-50 bombers await delivery on the south tarmac. The Meadows race track once stood near the far right end of the runway, very close to today's Museum of Flight. Renton Airport lies at the south end of Lake Washington on the upper left, with the still rural Kent Valley further south. Mt. Rainier dominates the scene—a crossroads of flying history in Seattle. *Copyright © Boeing, used with permission.*

Page 5 image: *Copyright © Boeing – used with permission.* See page 148 for caption.

Back cover image: *Copyright © Boeing – used with permission.* See page 34 for caption.

Type set in Kodchiang/ Times

ISBN: 978-0-7643-5106-8

Printed in China

Published by Schiffer Publishing, Ltd.
4880 Lower Valley Road | Atglen, PA 19310
Phone: (610) 593-1777; Fax: (610) 593-2002
E-mail: Info@schifferbooks.com
Web: www.schifferbooks.com

For our complete selection of fine books on this and related subjects, please visit our website at www.schifferbooks.com. You may also write for a free catalog.

Schiffer Publishing's titles are available at special discounts for bulk purchases for sales promotions or premiums. Special editions, including personalized covers, corporate imprints, and excerpts, can be created in large quantities for special needs. For more information, contact the publisher.

We are always looking for people to write books on new and related subjects. If you have an idea for a book, please contact us at proposals@schifferbooks.com.

DEDICATION

To Sean and Lisa—never fear to reach higher. To Debbie—who always supports
my hare-brained projects with unconditional love.

CONTENTS

FOREWORD

One of the most important advantages that has materialized as a result of having served at both the National Air and Space Museum and, more recently, the Museum of Flight has been a dawning perspective that I had frankly not anticipated. On reflection, and as I enter the late fall of my professional aviation history career, I have come to realize it is perhaps the most important of all. Stated simply, it is the recognition of what we are missing in our efforts to document the first full century of manned flight.

I have often said the history of manned flight has presented us with the first opportunity that we have ever had as a species to fully document one of mankind's greatest achievements because our ability to document these activities, both textually and photographically, matured at almost precisely the same time. I would like to report we are doing a good job, but the truth is we are already at risk of forever losing certain elements of the first pioneering epoch.

In this delightful and thoroughly enjoyable contribution to that literature, Tim Nelson has accomplished something that I can only hope others will repeat—not only in the United States, but world-wide. Although the nature of our love for aviation and aircraft is necessarily fluid and ever-changing, there is a crucial need for works of precisely this nature that enables us to conduct a check, at intervals, on where we are and, more importantly, where we have been and how we got there.

You will quickly recognize the sublime beauty of this compact tome rests in the fact that it can be enjoyed repeatedly and, quite aside from the pleasure of the first complete read-through, it will become a standard "go-to" reference for anyone studying the aviation history community of the Pacific Northwest and, in particular, the Puget Sound region.

If you love airplanes as Tim Nelson does, you are going to have a good time in these pages!

Dan Hagedorn
Curator and Director of Collections
The Museum of Flight at historic Boeing Field

ACKNOWLEDGMENTS

Even an eclectic, niche book project such as this prevails upon the kindness and expertise of many. At the pinnacle is the terrific curatorial and archives staff at The Museum of Flight in Seattle. I am indebted to Dan Hagedorn, John Little, Amy Heidrich, and Steve Ellis (docent and author) for their expert help, reviews, and sage counsel. Dan's mentorship on the publishing process was invaluable.

My heart-felt thanks also to the following:

Boeing corporate historian Mike Lombardi for key information and expert review, Mary Kane and Carlton Wilkerson at Boeing Images, and Keith Kurtz as a sanity checker

Sarah Frederick at the Eastside Heritage Center

Neal Pattison and Doug Parry at the *Everett Daily Herald*

Lisa Labovitch at the Everett Public Library

Cory Graff, Owen Richards, and Justin Spielmann at the Flying Heritage Collection

Mike True and Cara Cantonwine at the Fort Vancouver National Trust, caretakers of Pearson Field

Colleen Eastman and Gregg Munro at Kenmore Air

John Loacker at Kroll Map Company (an establishment whose history more than spans the time frame of this volume)

Jonathan Hall and Lashanna Williams at Lafarge Seattle, Jennifer Lewis at Lafarge North America

Carolyn Marr, Howard Giske, and Kathleen Knies at the Museum of History and Industry

Jeff Creighton at the Northwest Museum in Spokane

Scott Rook at the Oregon Historical Society in Portland

Ian Robertson at Schiffer Publishing for his patient tutelage.

Bob Dempster and John Hope at the Seattle World Cruiser Association

Jody Gripp at the Tacoma Public Library

Libby Hopfauf, Kris Kinsey, and Nicolette Bromberg at the University of Washington Libraries

Melanie Eastman and Tammy Moad at the Wenatchee Valley Museum

Ruth Steele at the Center for Pacific Northwest Studies, Western Washington University

Rebecca Wallick for advice and encouragement

A special acknowledgment to friends and colleagues in the Seattle area scale modeling community for their encouragement, photos, and/or reviews: Jim Schubert in particular, and Stephen Tontoni—who left us way too soon.

Any remaining errors after all of this help are squarely on my shoulders.

A final thank you to my family Debbie, Sean, and Lisa for encouragement, and tagging along on many obscure historical photo jaunts. I would be remiss not to acknowledge our golden retrieverish mutt Sam for always being there with a wink, a wag, a nod, and a smile.

Tim Nelson
Kirkland, Washington
July 2015

INTRODUCTION

An aviation enthusiast living in the Pacific Northwest in general, and in the Seattle area in particular, is a very lucky person indeed. From the dawn of human flight to today, this place has been host to flying history from dirigibles and fabric biplanes to jumbo jets… from epic pioneering flights to innovative companies making world travel routine. This book is intended to recapture a little of that historical awe and connect the reader with a sense of *place*. Some of the subjects span decades of existence and some represent a single day's events. Some are inspiring places of creativity and innovation, some are grim accident sites. All have some significance to the story of flight in the region.

This book is both an armchair history and a rough field guide. It is by no means a scholarly, deep-dive historical reference; others have covered many of these subjects in far more depth and detail. It relies heavily on secondary sources. However, I have attempted to provide a basic overview; enough to educate the new discoverer and satisfy the familiar student. The reader is encouraged to dig deeper in the many cited resources.

The material is organized—oddly it may seem for an aviation book—by location. Some helpful hints on how to find these sites— some easy, some a bit challenging—are shared. A relevant street address is listed, if such exists. Maps are included for general overview or historical purposes only. When contemplating a site visit, advance familiarization using Internet map/satellite tools is encouraged. In this era of ubiquitous and powerful smartphones, use of GPS navigation to a specific address is highly recommended. Unfortunately, no guarantee can be made that a site will remain as described or shown in these pages.

At some of these sites there is frankly nothing remaining to be seen. The passionate aviation enthusiast like you and me must be content knowing that you are *there*, regardless.

This book was researched and written between 2010 and 2015. Even during that short time the historical aviation landscape continued to evolve; for example, iconic Boeing Plant 2 was demolished (continued maintenance and hazmat concerns became untenable). Relentless development pressures will undoubtedly exert other changes. The reader attempting to visit these sites in the future will almost certainly encounter further significant change. Such is the nature of progress.

A book of this nature can only scratch the surface. Knowledgeable readers will no doubt have "*what about ___?!?*" moments. Apologies in advance for omissions of people, places, and museums near and dear to these readers.

My hope is that you will go and explore these places, let your mind ponder the remarkable events that took place there, and enjoy the journey.

CHAPTER ONE

SEATTLE, GEORGETOWN, AND TUKWILA

The industrial area south of Seattle includes gritty factories, shipyards, and warehouses. It is also rich in aviation lore, including the site of the first airplane flight in the state, the facilities that turned The Boeing Company into a global aviation power, one of the state's busiest airports (named for William E. Boeing), and one of the world's premier aerospace museums.

1. The Meadows Site (Modern South Boeing Field)
2. The Museum of Flight
3. Boeing Field
4. Gorst Field (Modern Lafarge North America cement plant)
5. Boeing Plant 1 Site
6. Boeing Plant 2 Site
7. Boeing Developmental Center
8. XB-29 Crash Site (1943)
9. B-50 Crash Site (1951)

(Copyright Kroll Map Company 2015, used with permission)

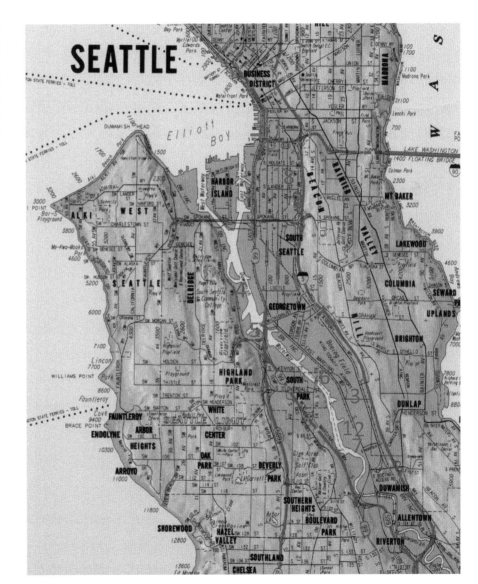

THE MEADOWS

Let's start with The Meadows, because it was the site of a singularly important aviation event—the first airplane flight in the state. You won't find this horse racing track and entertainment complex—it's been gone since the 1920s—but you will find plenty of interest nearby.

The Meadows track opened in 1902 and served as a venue for horse, auto, and even motorcycle racing. This large facility (seating 10,000 in the grandstands), including a hotel/resort, was a major attraction and source of entertainment during the short Northwest summer race season. Wagering was ubiquitous, and the surrounding saloons and other "establishments" benefited from the large crowds drawn to the area. The track was within a bend of the old, serpentine path of the Duwamish River, and was conveniently served by the major rail line running south from Seattle.[1] The Meadows was a natural site for a major public event and featured prominently in an earlier Seattle aviation first, when L. Guy Mecklem and his dirigible beat two cars to The Meadows in a race begun at Luna Park on July 4, 1908 (see chapter 3). It was an easy choice of venue for a pioneer barnstormer looking to show his stuff; enter Charles K. Hamilton.

Hamilton was known as the "Crazy Man of the Air" and was one of the earliest stunt fliers. He toured the USA in 1910, doing trick flying for the Curtiss Exhibition Company. These shows were witnessed by large crowds that mostly consisted of people seeing an airplane fly for the first time. Airplanes were obviously not common then, but the one Hamilton brought to Seattle that March was particularly special. It was the 1909 Herring-Curtiss No. 2 "Reims Racer" pusher designed by Glenn Curtiss, which won the first major international air race at Reims, France, in August 1909.[2] Flown by Curtiss himself, it went on to win similar events later in

Charles Hamilton, the "Crazy Man of the Air," at The Meadows in March 1910. (*UW Special Collections via The Museum of Flight*)

1909 in Brescia, Italy, and in January 1910 in Los Angeles (Dominguez Hills), California. These initial air meets proved hugely popular with the public and did much to spur the growth of aviation in these formative years. After these racing successes Curtiss leased the racer to Hamilton, who put it to use and abuse in his barnstorming tour. After test flights at The Meadows track on Friday, March 11, he began public flights on Saturday, March 12, which after enthralling the crowd of 10,000 with three flights ended abruptly with a crash in the infield pond. Fortunately, the impact did no lasting damage to either Hamilton or the airplane. However, he and his crew were unable to get the engine dried out and back in running condition and no further flying occurred that day.[3] The engine would not cooperate on Sunday either, resulting in no flights; this caused some irate reactions among the enthusiasts who came to see Hamilton fly (and possibly die). He appears to have gotten the airplane into the air twice on Monday before the engine balked again.

Hamilton moved on, but less well known is that he returned to the Seattle area a month later to fly with little fanfare on nearby Mercer Island.[4] Hamilton did other shows that March and April in Portland; Vancouver, BC; and Tacoma and Spokane before heading to the East Coast. He died four years later at age twenty-nine—not in a crash as many expected but of tuberculosis.[5]

The stimulating impact of Hamilton's flights at The Meadows can only be imagined. Given Seattle's subsequent major contributions to aviation, it is safe to assume the event had an inspiring effect on at least some individuals who later devoted their careers to this new industry. This would likely include future employees of a soon-to-be start-up airplane company founded by William Boeing.

A 1909 gambling ban in Washington was an eventual death sentence for The Meadows, but the facility persisted for some years as a public venue (apparently serving as a barn yard, among other things) until continuous industrial development, straightening of the Duwamish River, and the construction of Boeing Field forced its demolition.[6]

ABOVE

This image appears to capture Hamilton's first test flight at the Meadows on March 11, 1910. The view is east, toward Beacon Hill. The photo appears to have been taken from the south straight of the track oval, a location very close to today's Raisbeck Aviation High School. It was the first airplane flight in the area. (*UW Special Collections via The Museum of Flight*)

BELOW

The equivalent view in 2014, looking east from the general aviation ramp just north of The Museum of Flight. Rail lines still run along Airport Way on the east side of Boeing Field, at the base of Beacon Hill. (*Author*)

OPPOSITE

Well-dressed throngs thrill to Charles Hamilton's flights at The Meadows on March 12, 1910. (*UW Special Collections via The Museum of Flight*)

ABOVE

A panorama at the approximate site of The Meadows race track in March 2010, the centennial of Hamilton's flights. The Raisbeck Aviation High School now occupies much of this area just north of The Museum of Flight on East Marginal Way. (*Author*)

RIGHT

The author's scale model of the Curtiss "Reims Racer" as it might have looked in August 1909, when Glenn Curtiss flew it to victory in the world's first major air race at Reims, France. Race #8 is applied to the vertical fin. The very same aircraft was flown by Charles Hamilton at The Meadows seven months later. (*Author*)

Where exactly was The Meadows track? It occupied the area northwest of The Museum of Flight's main exhibit complex (1) shown on the adjacent map. The Meadows' grandstands were apparently on the south side of the oval, north of the Museum Aviation Pavilion (former Air Park, 2) and almost precisely where Raisbeck Aviation High School now stands (3). Stables and more viewing stands rimmed the north and west sides of the oval, in an area near the modern Insurance Auto Auctions facility (4) at 8801 East Marginal Way S. The oval extended east across modern East Marginal Way S (5) to today's general aviation hangars near Boeing Field runway 13R / 31L (6). As Charles Hamilton discovered, a large pond once stood in the infield of the oval.

Today no trace remains of The Meadows complex, but it can be imagined sprawling across the area north of The Museum of Flight. Patrons of the Museum's Wings Café can dine in the Meadows Room while gazing at numerous photos of Hamilton's historic flights. From there, the view north along the Boeing Field ramp takes in part of the site where The Meadows complex once stood, where crowds cheered and jeered a bold aviator and his Curtiss racer on a cold weekend in March 1910.

Former Site of The Meadows
(Just north of The Museum of Flight)
9404 East Marginal Way S
Seattle, WA

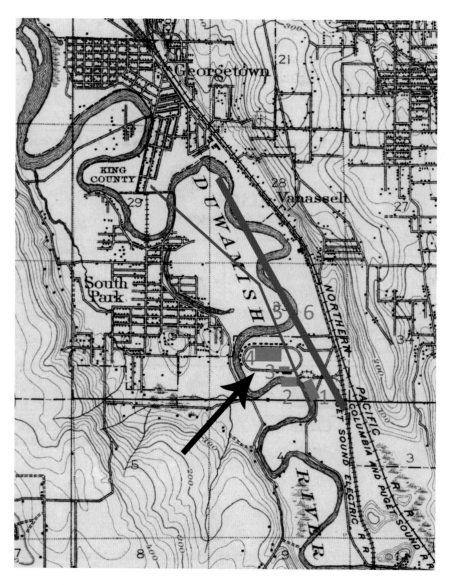

The Meadows oval can be clearly seen near the center of this 1909 map of Georgetown, South Park, and the Duwamish River valley. The river was rerouted and straightened in the 1920s. Modern features are overlaid by the author. Note the rail line to the east and the short spur delivering passengers to the track. (*US Geological Survey, Seattle, WA, 1909*. A 1992 USGS map of the area and satellite images were used to correlate the overlay.)

THE MUSEUM OF FLIGHT

It may seem odd to discuss an aviation museum at this point, but it makes sense for several reasons: The Museum of Flight (TMOF) resides among the many historical sites in this area, it includes a significant Boeing structure and several important Boeing subjects in its collection, and it's simply the premier air and space museum on the West Coast.

What became TMOF began as the Pacific Northwest Aviation Historical Foundation. The first exhibit space was at Seattle Center (site of the 1962 World's Fair), beginning in 1966. The move to the current location on East Marginal Way was enabled by saving The Boeing Company's "Red Barn" at Plant 1 and relocating the structure up the Duwamish River by barge. Fully restored, it was the first gallery of the current TMOF to open in 1983. The Great Gallery to the south opened in 1987, the J. Elroy McCaw Personal Courage Wing to the north opened in 2004, and the Charles Simonyi Space Gallery across East Marginal Way opened in 2012. The new Aviation Pavilion replaced the outdoor Air Park in 2016, between the Space Gallery and Raisbeck Aviation High School.[7] All of this lies within a short Curtiss pusher hop from the site of the old Meadows race track site.

TMOF includes in its vast collection the only surviving Boeing Model 80A-1, the first 727, the first 737 (in its later NASA markings), and the first 747. Its World War I and II fighter collections are world class.

The Museum library and archives are a treasure trove for researchers and enthusiasts alike. There is a sign hanging in the Reading Room of the Harl V. Brackin Library and Kenneth H. Dahlberg Center that nicely sums up the atmosphere: "Enthusiasts Welcome Here."

Plan on at least a full day enjoying all the museum has to offer. The Wings Café offers a fine selection of entrees and snacks with a sweeping view of busy Boeing Field.

The Museum of Flight
9404 East Marginal Way S
Seattle, WA 98108-4097
206-764-5720
www.museumofflight.org

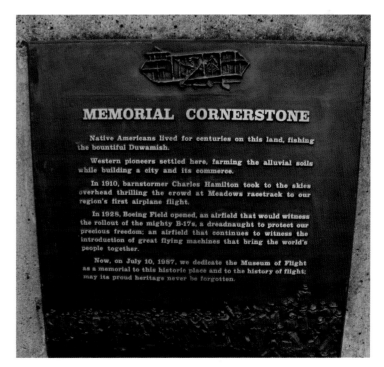

Cornerstone on The Museum's East Marginal Way entrance, acknowledging the 1910 Hamilton flights at the Meadows. (*Author*)

Boeing Model 80A-1 of 1929, which had the distinction of introducing the world's first female flight attendants, known as "stewardesses." This airplane is the last of its kind, rescued from an Alaskan junk yard in the 1960s. Its restoration was among the first projects taken on by the organization that became The Museum of Flight. (*Author*)

LEFT

The Red Barn from Boeing Plant 1 is the centerpiece of The Museum of Flight grounds. It features a history of The Boeing Company from its beginnings into the early jet age. It is an important artifact itself. The Great Gallery lies beyond. (*Author*)

BELOW

The Museum of Flight Wings Café Meadows Room pays homage to the 1910 Hamilton flights that took place practically right outside. (*Author*)

BOEING FIELD

Boeing Field is the unifying element in this immediate assemblage of sites in the Duwamish River valley. It is fitting that even in 1928, King County recognized the contributions of William E. Boeing by naming the area's first major airport after him and his still-young company. Other local airfields (Sand Point, Gorst, Camp Lewis) preceded it, but Boeing Field represented the region's first effort at a bona fide transport hub with a real passenger terminal, permanent hangars, and other facilities. The field opened on July 26, 1928, and continues to be an important aviation hub in the region.

This stretch of the Duwamish River valley was already historic as the location of early non-native settlers in the area, as well as The Meadows flights of 1910.[8] The establishment of Boeing Field ensured much history would unfold here for decades to come. Among the eventual results was the choice by Boeing in 1934 to locate its next major factory—to be known as Plant 2—on the northwest corner of the field. That facility would prove critical to the US industrial effort in World War II, producing thousands of Boeing B-17 Flying Fortress bombers; it was demolished in 2011. We will take a closer look at Plant 2 and its predecessor farther north along the Duwamish River in subsequent pages.

West of the midpoint of Boeing Field, near the FAA control tower, is the Boeing Transonic Wind Tunnel (BTWT, pronounced "bitwit" within the company). Boeing established this facility in 1941, and has continually upgraded it to the state of the art ever since.[9] The swept wing B-47 was the first major design to be extensively tested here, and every major Boeing jet has been shaped to some extent within its test section. The facility was formally named the Edmund T. Allen Wind Tunnel and Aeronautical Research Laboratories in the wake of the XB-29 accident that claimed Allen's life in 1943. Its importance to the company's fortunes after World War II cannot be overstated. BTWT is not open to the public.

SIGNIFICANT FIRST FLIGHTS AT BOEING FIELD[10]

Boeing Monomail (May 22, 1930), Eddie Allen

Boeing B-9 (April 29, 1931), Les Tower

Boeing P-26 (March 10, 1932), Les Tower

Boeing 247 (February 8, 1933), Les Tower and Louis Goldsmith

Boeing Model 299, B-17 Prototype (July 28, 1935), Les Tower, Louis Wait, and Henry Igo

Boeing XB-15 (October 15, 1937), Eddie Allen, Maj. Johnny Corkille, and Mike Pavone

Boeing 307 (December 31, 1938), Eddie Allen, Julius Barr, Earl Ferguson, and others

Boeing B-29 (September 21, 1942), Eddie Allen, A. C. Reed, W. F. Milliken, and others

Boeing C-97 (November 9, 1944), Elliott Merrill and John Fornasero

Boeing 377 (July 8, 1947), John Fornasero, Robert Lamson, and N. D. Showalter

Boeing B-47 (December 17, 1947), Bob Robbins and Scott Osler

Boeing B-52 (April 15, 1952), Tex Johnston and Lt. Col. Guy Townsend

Boeing 737 (April 9, 1967), Brien Wygle and Lew Wallick

Boeing YC-14 (August 9, 1976), Ray McPherson and Maj. David Bittenbinder

From the late 1930s to the present day, the north end of Boeing Field has been dominated by Boeing Flight Test. The commercial operation is still there, where test airplanes and new 737s prepping for delivery are a common sight on the Boeing ramp. The south end is home to the military side, where 737 variants such as the P-8 Poseidon and other types bristling with antennae can be seen. The best vantage point to view these ever-changing flight lines is actually the various aviation facilities along Airport Way S on the east side of the airport.

The original King County International Airport passenger terminal still exists on the east side of Boeing Field, restored in all its art deco glory. Emblematic of this hard-working airport, it is fully functional, used by Kenmore Air and others in daily operation.

King County Airport Terminal
7277 Perimeter Rd. S
Seattle WA 98108
(206) 296-7431
www.kingcounty.gov/transportation/kcdot/Airport.aspx

A steady presence on the north tip of the airport, visible in countless photos taken here over the decades, is the Georgetown Steam Plant. The plant opened in 1906 and operated until 1972. It is on the National Register of Historic Places and is well preserved as the Georgetown PowerPlant Museum. Open hours are limited, so be sure to check before you go:

Georgetown PowerPlant Museum
6605 13th Ave. S
Seattle, WA 98108
(206) 763-2542
www.seattle.gov/light/georgetownsteamplant

RIGHT

Boeing Field dedication plaque from the field's opening in 1928. The plaque is installed in the east parking lot of the King County Airport terminal. (*Author*)

Boeing Field tours are typically available during summer months at The Museum of Flight and by arrangement with the King County International Airport authority.

No visit to Boeing Field is complete without dining at Randy's Restaurant. Boeing employees, aviation buffs, and even the US Navy Blue Angels frequent this warm and friendly diner that is filled to the rafters with flying memorabilia. Open 24 hours!

Randy's Restaurant
10016 E Marginal Way S
Tukwila, WA 98168
(206) 763-9333
www.randys-restaurant.net

Boeing Field aerial view looking to the west, July 1934. The King County Airport terminal, which opened in 1930, can be seen near the center of the photograph, with the Boeing and United hangars to the left. The Georgetown steam plant is at upper right. Boeing's Plant 2 would soon take shape on the near banks of the Duwamish River at upper left. (*The Boeing Company Collection at The Museum of Flight*)

LEFT

Boeing Field terminal in the mid-1930s, with a United Air Lines Boeing 247 and a Canadian Airways de Havilland DH.89 Dragon Rapide. (*The Museum of Flight Collection*)

BELOW

A similar view of the much-remodeled Boeing Field (King County Airport) terminal in 2013. A Kenmore Air Cessna 208 Caravan awaits passengers and cargo. (*Author*)

Another aerial view from the late 1930s, showing the terminal on the lower left, with Boeing and United hangars on the right. B-17C airplanes await attention at Boeing while a 247 rests at United. A single Waco YKS-7 cabin biplane of the US Bureau of Commerce is parked near the terminal. The terminal and the warehouse/office building at the upper left, along Airport Way, still stand. (*The Boeing Company Collection at The Museum of Flight*)

RIGHT

The east side of the terminal in 2013. The building was completely restored in 2003, and features a wonderful art deco interior. (*Author*)

BELOW

Roughly west across the runways from the terminal, on the west side of East Marginal Way, is the Boeing Transonic Wind Tunnel. This cutaway diagram dates to the opening of the facility in the early 1940s. The test circuit, main fan, and multiple turning vanes can be seen at upper left. The complex, which test pilot Eddie Allen urged the company to create, has been continually upgraded and is still in use as of this writing. (*The Boeing Company Collection at The Museum of Flight*)

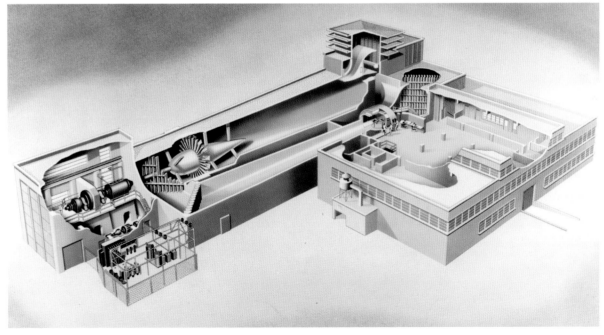

RIGHT

The modern FAA tower, seismically reinforced after the February 2001 Nisqually earthquake, has a commanding view of the busy activities at Boeing Field. Across East Marginal Way to the west is the Boeing Transonic Wind Tunnel facility. The spherical tanks are associated with the companion supersonic wind tunnel. (*Author*)

BELOW

A B-52D, the very first KC-135 tanker, two 707-300 test aircraft, 707s for TWA and BOAC, and a C-135 transport share the north Boeing Field flight line in the summer of 1958. The Georgetown steam plant looms in the distance. Part of the large flight test hangar complex called the "B-52 Hangar" can be seen protruding on the left. The facility is still very much in use in the twenty-first century. (Note: B-52D 56-0591 in the foreground was named "Tommy's Tigator" and monitored hydrogen bomb tests at Bikini Atoll. The Wichita-built aircraft was in Seattle at the time of the photo for low altitude bomb delivery testing. The aircraft was lost with five company personnel on a test mission in eastern Oregon on June 23, 1959.[11] (*The Boeing Company Collection at The Museum of Flight*)

A view in the opposite direction, late summer 2013. Boeing 787 test aircraft, including
the first 787-9, are seen along with multiple 737s farther south. The FAA tower can be seen
about a mile to the south. Mt. Rainier looms majestically on the horizon. (*Author*)

RIGHT

The hangar on the far northwest corner of Boeing Field was part of the Boeing Flying Fortress School in World War II. Known as "Hangar 1" or the "B-17 Hangar," it is seen here with the prototype Boeing XB-52 still under wraps for a modicum of secrecy in this circa 1952 photo. (*The Boeing Company Collection at The Museum of Flight*)

BELOW

The hangar exists today and is still in use. This view is from the east side of Boeing Field, across the runways. (*Author*)

The Georgetown Steam Plant has been a fixture in the area that became Boeing Field since 1906.
Although its tall smokestacks are long gone it has been preserved and is currently a museum. (*Author*)

GORST FIELD

Like The Meadows race track, Gorst Field has not actually existed for many decades, but this little patch of real estate was home to the first commercial air operation in the Seattle area with far-reaching implications.

When the US Post Office opened bidding for private contractors to take over air mail under the Kelly Act of 1925, several entrepreneurs were ready to strike. Among these was Vern Gorst, who established Pacific Air Transport (PAT), with the aircraft and infrastructure needed to fly the demanding Seattle-Los Angeles route. Initially based at Sand Point on Lake Washington, PAT moved the air mail operation to a site closer to downtown that became known as PAT Airport or Gorst Field. Nicknamed the "Sand Lot," this 1,800-foot long runway was Seattle's first and primary commercial airport until yielding to nearby Boeing Field in 1928.[12]

Gorst initially operated a fleet of pure mailplanes, featuring Ryan M-1s. A Fokker Universal that could accommodate five or six passengers in addition to the more profitable load of mail was added later. In 1928, Gorst sold his interest in PAT to Bill Boeing, whose own Boeing Air Transport (BAT) was flying the San Francisco-Chicago mail route with revolutionary Boeing Model 40As.[12] In 1930, Gorst played a role in the integration of BAT, PAT, and Varney Air Lines into United Air Lines. (The evolution, integration, and forced breakup of these companies, along with Boeing and Pratt & Whitney, is a long, convoluted, and fascinating story well beyond our scope.)

Gorst Field also served as one of several flight test sites for Boeing aircraft of the 1920s. The airplanes had to be trucked from the nearby Duwamish/Oxbow Factory (later known as Plant 1) before they could take to the air.

After the opening of Boeing Field, Gorst's Sand Lot fell into disuse and was redeveloped. The current Lafarge cement plant on the site was built in 1966. A small fountain commemorates the location's aviation heritage. During plant open hours you can drive in, park, and take a look. This is a busy industrial site, so use caution and be aware of large vehicles coming and going.

Lafarge North America
5400 W Marginal Way SW
Seattle WA 98106
(206) 937-8025

The Lafarge North America cement plant on the historical site of Gorst Field. A small memorial fountain acknowledging the location of Gorst Field lies in a covered plaza just to the right of this view. (*Author*)

Vern Gorst's Pacific Air Transport (PAT) Fokker Universal at Gorst Field, also known as PAT Airport, in 1927. The pilot awaits his passengers under the Fokker's wing; no more than six of this eclectic crowd will be able to fly (and probably less with a load of air mail). (*The Museum of Flight Collection*)

LEFT

The same perspective in 2014, from the Lafarge parking lot looking west across West Marginal Way. (*Author*)

BELOW

Memorial fountain commemorating Gorst Field and the first commercial air service in Seattle at the Lafarge cement plant. (*Author*)

BELOW RIGHT

Closeup of the fountain plaque, "…dedicated to the nation's pioneer commercial air mail pilots…" It was installed in 1966 to recognize the 40th anniversary of commercial air mail service to Seattle. (*Author*)

BOEING PLANT 1

What became Boeing Plant 1 originated as the Heath Shipyard on the Duwamish River and was acquired by Bill Boeing in 1910, when his main business was lumber. He may have been partially motivated to ensure the shipyard remained solvent enough to build his yacht, the *Taconite*! When his quickly expanding airplane business outgrew its Lake Union hangar in 1917, the Heath facility was a logical next location.[14] The building later known as the "Red Barn" was part of the original Heath facility.

Known as the Oxbow or Duwamish plant, the factory space grew with a series of additions over the ensuing twenty years. During the post World War I years when the airplane business was lean, Boeing built furniture and boats at Oxbow, but it was here that the Boeing Airplane Company transformed from a local start-up venture to a trusted and world famous aircraft manufacturer. By the late 1930s, bursting at the seams with fighter and huge flying boat production, Boeing built another factory adjacent to Boeing Field known as "Plant 2." Like the world wars of this same era, the first factory then gained the moniker "Plant 1" after the fact.

Some of the significant Boeing types to be manufactured at the Oxbow factory (Plant 1) include:[15]

Model C (Navy seaplane trainer)

Curtiss HS-2L (license production contract)

B-1 flying boat (just one built)

de Havilland DH-4M (refurbishment of the army fleet, replaced original wood structure with welded steel tubing)

PW-9 (the company's first pursuit [fighter] type, sold to the US Army)

Model 40 (the company's first mass-produced commercial model and a major enabler of successful air mail and passenger service in the US)

Model 80 (the company's first purpose-built passenger airliner)

F4B / P-12 series (hugely successful fighter aircraft of the 1930s)

Monomail (advanced all-metal monoplane, final wing/body join at Boeing Field)

B-9 (advanced twin engine all-metal bomber, nicknamed "Death Angel")

P-26 Peashooter (advanced all-metal monoplane fighter)

247 (advanced twin-engine airliner)

Model 299 (prototype of the B-17 Flying Fortress, one of the most important aircraft of World War II. Some early B-17 production work also occurred here)

XB-15 (large bomber prototype; due to its enormous size major assemblies were barged to Plant 2 for final assembly)

314 Clipper (the largest of the Pan American flying boats; wings were fabricated at Plant 2 and barged to Plant 1 for final assembly outdoors)

With the shift in production to Plant 2 after 1936, Plant 1 continued to serve as a fabrication facility for parts and subassemblies. It was also home to the company's small gas turbine and jet engine business from the mid-1940s until 1969. By the late 1960s, the old factory's days were numbered. Boeing sold the property to the Port of Seattle in 1970, where it was redeveloped into today's massive Terminal 115 complex.

Boeing's Oxbow / Duwamish River complex, later known as Plant 1, seen from the air in this mid-1920s photo. The 1st Avenue South Bridge crosses the Duwamish in the foreground and West Marginal Way curves around the back of the facility. (*The Boeing Company Collection at The Museum of Flight*)

Only two buildings survive from the Boeing era at Plant 1: one of them is on site, a remodeled brick office structure that once served as an engineering and administrative center.[16] From here, it is still possible to imagine the neighboring clap-trap assemblage of factory buildings along the Duwamish River and the important Boeing aircraft that emerged here.

Former Plant 1 Site
200 SW Michigan St.
Seattle WA 98106

The other survivor is Building 5 (later 105), more commonly known as the Red Barn, relocated up the Duwamish River in the 1970s to Boeing Field and now a major part of The Museum of Flight. Today, the Red Barn is filled with artifacts telling the story of Boeing's first fifty years and provides a firsthand feel for the environment of aircraft design and manufacture in the early days of flight (see more under "The Museum of Flight").

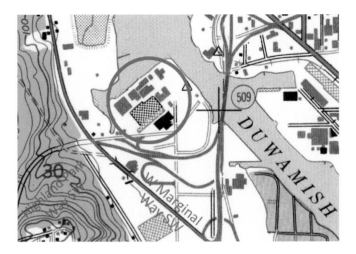

This 1949 map shows the Plant 1 facility past its prime but still in use. The 200 SW Michigan St. building is shaded black. The Red Barn is the second magenta building from the left. (*US Geological Survey (Seattle South, WA 1949)*)

This model at The Museum of Flight provides a three-dimensional perspective of the historical Plant 1 site in its early years as a Boeing facility. The model is on display inside the Red Barn itself, saved and relocated from Plant 1 to the current museum location in 1975. (*Author*)

Boeing Model 40s in various stages of assembly at Plant 1 in 1927. The Model 40A was Boeing's first successful commercial aircraft and a mainstay of Boeing's own air mail company. The biplane had a crew of one, two compartments for mail, and a small cabin for two passengers. Two TB-1 torpedo bombers for the US Navy take shape on the right. (*Copyright © Boeing, used with permission*)

LEFT

Boeing Model 80A airliners and F4B-1 fighters for the US Navy share factory space at Plant 1 in 1927. These increasingly cramped conditions were one of several motivations for a new and larger factory adjacent to Boeing Field. Another issue was flight test and delivery; airplanes had to be disassembled, crated, and trucked or barged to other locations such as Sand Point and Gorst Field, then reassembled. (*Copyright © Boeing, used with permission*)

BELOW

The Boeing Model 80 series, constructed at Plant 1, was the company's first purpose built passenger airliner with comfortable seating for twelve (later expanded to eighteen). Two additional vertical fins were installed during flight test. The early 80A shown here is soaring over the Lake Washington Ship Canal, with Lake Union in the distance. The Gas Works (now a park) can be seen immediately left of the aircraft's nose. Sharp-eyed observers may spot the old Boeing Lake Union hangar on the far shore beyond the Gas Works. (*Copyright © Boeing, used with permission*)

RIGHT

In 1930, Boeing Air Transport Model 80As introduced aviation's first stewardesses (one per airplane). The women shown here were the "original eight" hired and were required to be registered nurses. Boeing Air Transport would later become part of United Airlines. (*Copyright © Boeing, used with permission*)

BELOW

The Boeing Monomail 221A in company colors, demonstrating passenger loading near the Boeing Field terminal circa 1931. Two Monomails were built at Plant 1: the Model 200 mail plane and the Model 221 six-passenger transport. Both were subsequently revised for transcontinental passenger service and designated Model 221As. Although not commercially successful, this pair of airplanes was one of the most significant and influential designs in aviation history. Contrast the design features (smooth all-metal construction, cantilevered low wing monoplane configuration, drag reducing engine cowling, and retracting landing gear) with the Model 80 of only three years before. One of the Monomails would conduct an experiment definitively showing the performance benefit of retractable landing gear—heavier but aerodynamically clean—over then-standard fixed gear. (*Copyright © Boeing, used with permission*)

LEFT

The Boeing Model 215 (YB-9 bomber prototype) as it appeared at Boeing Field before first flight in the spring of 1931; the design influences of the recent Monomail are evident. Although the larger US Army Air Corps order went to the Martin B-10, the Boeing B-9 emerged from Plant 1 as a quantum leap in large airplane design that would reverberate throughout the 1930s and early 1940s. (*The Boeing Company Collection at The Museum of Flight*)

BELOW

The world of the 1930s was not actually grayscale. The author's scale model of the same airplane is shown here in the striking company colors of the era: Boeing Green, Boeing Gray (a greenish gray), and International Orange. (*Author*)

The prototype B-17 Flying Fortress (the Model 299) debuted in July 1935. Built at Plant 1 and reassembled at Boeing Field, it is seen here at its unveiling at the Boeing hangar on the east side of Boeing Field. Note what appears to be a Sikorsky S-39 in the hangar. (*The Boeing Company Collection at The Museum of Flight*)

The Model 299 is posed with another Plant 1 product: two Boeing P-26 Peashooter fighters. The Boeing Field terminal can be seen in the background. (*The Boeing Company Collection at The Museum of Flight*)

Boeing 314 Clipper NC-18606, which would be christened *American Clipper* by Pan American Airways, can be seen awaiting finishing touches at Building 8 in this 1939 photo of the Plant 1 facility. Expansion of the plant over the previous twenty years is evident. Although the production space was cramped, easy access to the Duwamish River had its advantages for the big flying boats. The "Red Barn" lies just to the left of the Clipper. The brick structure on the far right, with the double sawtooth roof, still survives on the site. In the hazy distance to the east the Georgetown steam plant and Boeing Field can be seen. This hillside viewpoint is a dense woods today, but is in the vicinity of Riverview Playfield and South Seattle College in the Riverview neighborhood. (*The Boeing Company Collection at The Museum of Flight*)

The elegant Boeing 314 Clipper series was perhaps the most famous aircraft to emerge from Plant 1. Here NC-18606—too large to be indoors at this stage—is in final assembly on the Duwamish River outside Plant 1, May 15, 1939. (*The Peter M. Bowers Collection / The Museum of Flight*)

The Clippers were towed from Plant 1 north (downstream) to Elliott Bay for testing. Here Boeing Chief Test Pilot Eddie Allen poses with a Clipper on Seattle's Elliott Bay in 1938. Allen was considered one of the world's top test pilots but would lose his life in the tragic XB-29 accident in February 1943. (*The Boeing Company Collection at The Museum of Flight*)

ABOVE

The Boeing 314 Clipper featured amenities to pamper transoceanic travelers, including a full dining room and aviation's first flushable toilets. Pan Am's Clippers were configured for luxury—there was no "coach" section. (*The Boeing Company Collection at The Museum of Flight*)

RIGHT

The Clipper also offered train-style Pullman sleeping berths. (*The Boeing Company Collection at The Museum of Flight*)

LEFT

One of the great injustices of aviation is the fact that not a single Boeing 314 Clipper was preserved. The Museum of Flight does have two remnants: a trim tab and an anchor. (A partial replica 314 was created for the Foynes Flying Boat & Maritime Museum near Shannon International Airport in Ireland.) (*Author*)

BELOW LEFT

The brick building at 200 SW Michigan St. is the last surviving structure from the Boeing era still at the Plant 1 site. It was built as an engineering and administration building in 1929, in response to the company's growing needs. It occupies the southeast corner of the former Plant 1 site. (*Author*)

BELOW RIGHT

Port of Seattle Terminal 115 occupies the site where the bulk of Plant 1 once stood, sprawling behind the 200 SW Michigan St. building. This 2015 view is looking west back toward the Riverview hill from which the 1939 image with Boeing 314 *American Clipper* was taken. (*Author*)

BOEING PLANT 2

The challenges of operation at Boeing's Oxbow plant (later called Plant 1) were becoming untenable by the mid-1930s. Cramped production, antiquated tooling, and no adjacent airport were all factors that led Boeing to seek a new facility. What became Plant 2 on the north end of Boeing Field next to the Duwamish River would solve all of these problems.

The initial factory space at Plant 2 was state of the art for 1936. In the coming years it would expand several times over and come to symbolize the industrial might of wartime America.

Significant types manufactured at Plant 2 include:[17]

XB-15 (large bomber prototype [final assembly]; although not mass produced, it gave the company important experience in large aircraft design and production)

307 Stratoliner (first airliner with a pressurized cabin)

Douglas DB-7 (A-20 variant, under license)

B-17 Flying Fortress (almost 7,000 produced here during World War II; a similar number elsewhere under license)

XB-29/YB-29 Superfortress prototypes (three aircraft; some fabrication at Plant 1)

B-29 subassemblies (assembled in Renton)

B-50 (advanced postwar version of the B-29)

C-97 (advanced postwar military transport developed from B-29; production later moved to Renton)

377 Stratocruiser (advanced postwar airliner developed from the B-29)

XB-47 Stratojet (two prototypes of the first swept-wing jet, a quantum leap in bomber performance; some fabrication at Plant 1, but production was in Wichita, KS)

B-52 Stratofortress (prototypes and early production of this famous bomber still serving in the twenty-first century)

737 (prototype and initial airframes; early production of the world's most popular airliner was at the Thompson Site about a mile south; the vast majority of production was in Renton)

By the 1970s, significant aircraft production work had moved to other facilities. The vast and mostly idle space still served as a home to various aircraft restoration projects, including the Model 367-80, The Museum of Flight B-17F, and the Seattle World Cruiser project (see chapter 4), until 2010. By this time the facility had deteriorated far beyond economic repair, complicated by several decades' accumulation of hazardous waste. Following demolition of the complex in 2011, Boeing financed a restoration of the Duwamish shoreline to its pre-industrial state.

Sweeping views of the former Plant 2 location can be had from the west side of the Duwamish River at the South Park Marina.

South Park Marina
8604 Dallas Ave. S
Seattle, WA 98108

The old Boeing corporate headquarters building remains on the site along E Marginal Way, serving that purpose until the corporate organization moved to Chicago in 2001.

Former Boeing Corporate Headquarters Site
7755 East Marginal Way S
Tukwila, WA 98108

Boeing Plant 2 has already undergone one expansion in this late 1930s aerial view; it would grow much more during the World War II years. Three Boeing 307 Stratoliners are in work outside, adjacent to East Marginal Way. Wartime B-17 production would soon dominate the proceedings here. In the background, the 14th Ave. "South Park" bridge spans the Duwamish River. (*The Boeing Company Collection at The Museum of Flight*)

RIGHT

The Boeing Model 294—better known as the XB-15—
resembled the B-17, but was a much larger aircraft. It was a
product of both Plants 1 (subassemblies) and 2 (final assembly),
rolling out in 1937. It never entered production, but design
lessons—and its wings—were applied to the 314 Clipper. The
XB-15 rests here next to Boeing's hangar just south of the main
Boeing Field terminal. The distinctive hangar is long gone; this
area is now an air freight center. (*The Boeing Company
Collection at The Museum of Flight*)

BELOW

The XB-15—nicknamed "Grand
Pappy"—flies over Lake Union and
Portage Bay. The University of
Washington campus and the
horseshoe of Husky Stadium can be
seen directly beneath the mammoth
aircraft. Union Bay and Lake
Washington lie beyond. (*The Boeing
Company Collection at The Museum
of Flight*)

Boeing B-17D Flying Fortresses nearing completion outside an expanding Plant 2 circa 1941. East Marginal Way runs to the left of the image. The B-17D incorporated self-sealing fuel tanks, more armor protection, and increased armament; all lessons learned by the British Royal Air Force in early fighting against Germany. (*Copyright © Boeing, used with permission*)

ABOVE

Wartime demands drove B-17 production at Plant 2 to legendary proportions. Almost 7,000 Flying Fortresses were manufactured here during 1941–45, with a B-17 rolling out every ninety minutes at the peak rate. (*The Boeing Company Collection at The Museum of Flight*)

RIGHT

The faux streets crisscrossing the ersatz neighborhood atop the Plant 2 roof even had names befitting their authenticity. (*The Boeing Company Collection at The Museum of Flight*)

Boeing's Plant 2 was famously disguised during the war years under a fake urban camouflage.
After the war, the odd scene was allowed to be photographed. The Duwamish River is on the right, spanned
by the 14th Ave. S "South Park" Bridge. (*The Boeing Company Collection at The Museum of Flight*)

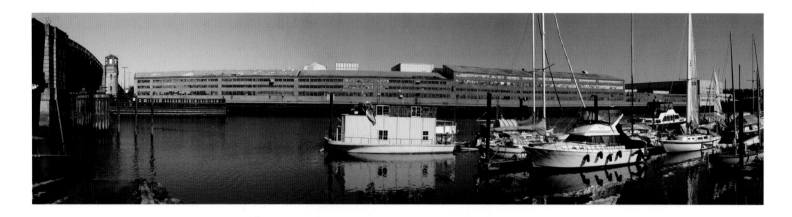

ABOVE

A panorama of Plant 2 in 2010, shortly before its demolition, from the South Park Marina area on the west side of the Duwamish River. The old, original 14th Avenue S "South Park" bridge is at left. (*Author*)

RIGHT

The Plant 2 site in 2014, seen from same location. After its demolition in 2010–11, Boeing restored the area to its pre-industrial natural state. A rebuilt South Park bridge now spans the river. The white structure now visible across the river is the former Boeing corporate headquarters complex, used for other company purposes after corporate offices relocated to Chicago in 2001. (*Author*)

BOEING DEVELOPMENTAL CENTER

The Developmental Center—more commonly known as the "DC"—is among Boeing's most secretive facilities, despite being in plain sight along East Marginal Way.

The DC dates to 1957 and has hosted a plethora of engineering programs within its opaque walls. Significant projects or manufacturing efforts here include:[18]

Bomarc missile

Minuteman Intercontinental Ballistic Missile (ICBM)

X-20 Dyna-Soar

Supersonic Transport (SST)

MX Peacekeeper ICBM

YC-14 Short Takeoff and Landing prototypes

E-3A Airborne Warning and Control (AWACS) modifications

Northrop B-2 Spirit stealth bomber subassemblies

X-32 Joint Strike Fighter (JSF) prototype

Lockheed F-22 Raptor subassemblies

777 and 787 subassemblies

and more that we can't discuss…

> **Boeing Developmental Center**
> 9725 East Marginal Way S
> Seattle, WA

About a half mile north along East Marginal Way is a large, white, boxy structure known as the Thompson Site. The first 737s were produced here, and it later served as the engine buildup facility for airplanes being produced in Renton and Everett. In the years following 2010 the site went full circle, becoming the location for installation of military equipment on 737s destined to become P-8 Poseidon aircraft for the US Navy and other countries.[19] As you might expect, none of these facilities are open to the public.

The DC in the late 1960s, with a Supersonic Transport profile visible on its north side. (*The Boeing Company Collection at The Museum of Flight*)

The DC from E Marginal Way in 2013, including the "12" flag representing the rabid fans of the NFL's Seattle Seahawks. (*Author*)

XB-29 CRASH SITE

The Boeing B-29 was developed and tested in secrecy, under wartime pressure to develop a long-range bomber far more capable than the B-17 already in service. Design began in 1940, when the imminent need for such a weapon was becoming readily apparent. First flight was conducted from Boeing Field on September 21, 1942.

In the late 1930s and early 1940s, Boeing Chief Pilot Eddie Allen was perhaps the most highly regarded test pilot in the world. He strongly influenced the design and led the testing of major Boeing types of the era, such as the B-17 and 314 Clipper. It was Allen who was pilot in command of that first flight of the XB-29.[20] Two XB-29 prototypes carried the load in the early test phase, followed by a third aircraft designated YB-29.

XB-29 with test pilot Eddie Allen after the first taxi test in September 1942. (*Copyright © Boeing, used with permission*)

The B-29 was a giant technological leap forward from the B-17 that first flew only seven years before. In addition to a pressurized cabin and remotely operated gun turrets, the B-29 flew higher, faster, and farther, with a bigger bomb load. But it was the equally cutting edge Wright R-3350 engines that threatened to derail the program.

Flight testing during the winter of 1942–43 was plagued with engine problems, most notably a tendency to overheat. The first flight of the second XB-29 in December 1942 was cut short by an engine fire. On February 18, 1943, the same aircraft suffered an engine fire after departure from Boeing Field. Eddie Allen was again at the controls and made a valiant attempt to return to land at Boeing Field. With the fire out of control, the XB-29 could not make it and crashed into the Frye Meat Packing Plant in south Seattle. Allen and the crew of ten were killed (two of the crew bailed out but struck the ground), along with at least nineteen employees of the Frye plant.[21]

XB-29 Crash Site (former Frye Meat Packing Plant)
2203 Airport Way S
Seattle, WA

Boeing named its transonic wind tunnel facility at Boeing Field in Eddie Allen's honor, and his name is still revered in the flight test community.

The B-29 would go on to play an enormous role in winning the war in the Pacific. Almost 4,000 airplanes were delivered by the end of the war in August 1945, with most of the units produced in nearby Renton and in Wichita, Kansas.

ABOVE

Fires rage at the Frye Meat Packing Plant following the crash of the Boeing XB-29 on February 18, 1943. Note the firemen and pigs silhouetted in the distance on the right. (*Museum of History and Industry*)

RIGHT

The Frye site in 2012 viewed from South Walker St. The building now houses the Washington State Patrol Crime Lab and other local government offices, and is said to have been built on the Frye plant foundation. The lobby contains photographs commemorating the awful day in 1943. (*Author*)

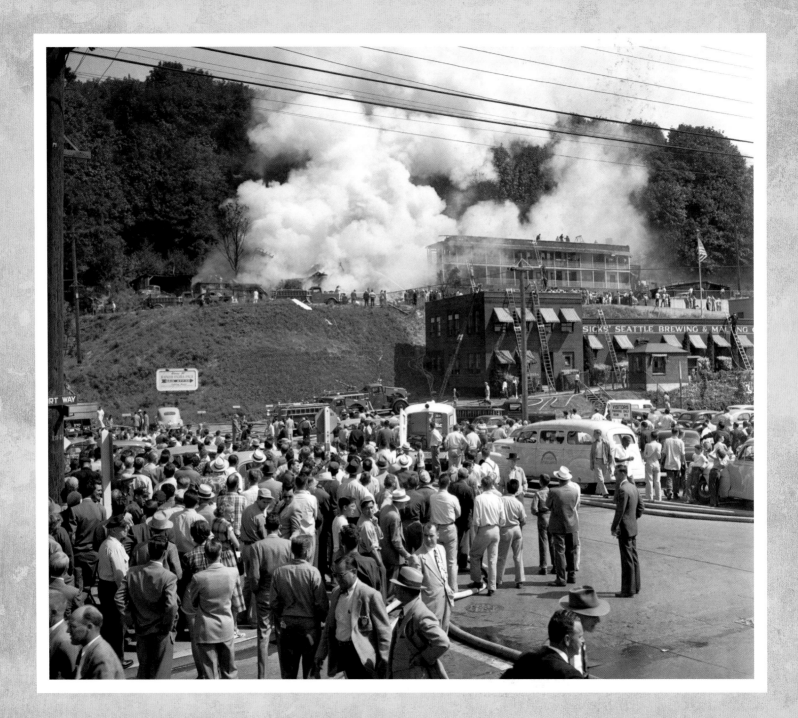

B-50 CRASH SITE

The Boeing B-50 was a later development of the B-29. This particular aircraft was on a test flight on August 13, 1951, following modifications. While departing northbound from Boeing Field, it developed engine trouble and crashed into the Lester Apartments adjacent to Sicks' Brewing & Malting Company. The accident claimed the lives of all six personnel on board and five persons on the ground. It also destroyed the Lester Apartments complex, infamous in its past as perhaps the world's largest bordello.[22]

The Sicks' Brewing complex survives in the form of the Old Rainier Brewery, used by Rainier Brewing for decades before becoming Tully's Coffee headquarters in 2000. In 2013, a replica of the famous Rainier "R" logo was reinstalled atop the old brewery building. (This location is barely a quarter-mile south of the 1943 XB-29 crash site at 2203 Airport Way.)

B-50 Crash Site
The Old Rainier Brewery
3100 Airport Way S
Seattle, WA 98134
(206) 650-9437
www.theoldrainierbrewery.com

The crash site near the Old Rainier Brewery, 2014. The Sicks' Seattle Brewing building is now behind the brick structure in the foreground. Interstate 5 runs over the actual crash site in the background. (*Author*)

OPPOSITE

Crowd gathered after the B-50 crash at the Lester Apartments, Seattle, August 13, 1951. (*Museum of History and Industry*)

CHAPTER TWO

SEATTLE, LAKE UNION

Seattle's Lake Union is a roughly "Y"-shaped fresh water lake north of downtown. It is bounded by the Queen Anne Hill, Fremont, Wallingford, Eastlake, and South Lake Union neighborhoods. Known for seaplanes, sailing, Gas Works Park vistas, and a large houseboat community, it has a major claim to fame as the place where The Boeing Company began. Its south shore witnessed explosive business growth and redevelopment in the early twenty-first century.

1. Birthplace of Boeing Site
2. Kurtzer Terminal Site (Modern Kenmore Air Seaplane Terminal)
3. Museum of History and Industry
4. Gas Works Park

(Copyright Kroll Map Company 2015, used with permission)

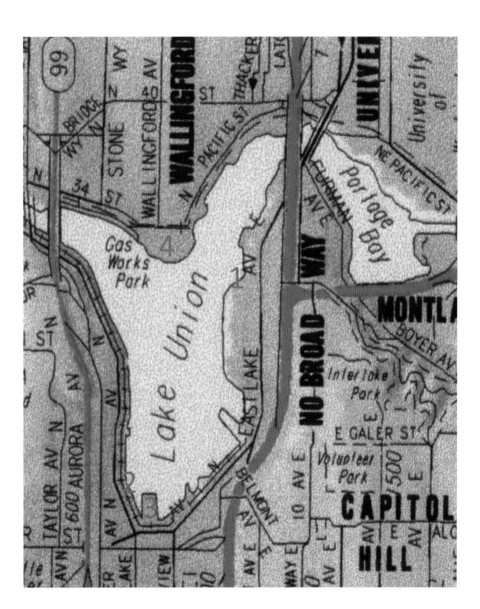

LAKE UNION

The Boeing Company, which in the early twenty-first century stands like an aerospace colossus astride the globe, had inauspicious beginnings in a small seaplane hangar on the eastern shore of Lake Union. The hangar was built in 1915, instigated by William E. Boeing as the home of the Aero Club of the Northwest, a flying enthusiast group.[1] Boeing and Conrad Westervelt started the Pacific Aero Products Company in July 1916, and their first design, the B&W (Boeing & Westervelt), emerged from this facility in June of that year. Within a year, the company was renamed the Boeing Airplane Company and had outgrown this location.[2] It found a suitable new home on the Duwamish River, later known as "Plant 1," where Bill Boeing—who despite his lumber and businessman background would exert a profound influence on early aviation—could realize his vision.

Significant types manufactured at the Lake Union hangar and which first flew off Lake Union include:[3]

B&W (Model 1; only two built named "Bluebill" and "Mallard")

Model C (fifty trainers sold to the US Navy; initial production before shifting to the Duwamish Plant)

Boeing continued to retain the Lake Union facility for seaplane operations—by the company and others—for decades. Of significant note, the hangar was the terminus for the first international air mail flight from Victoria, BC, flown by Eddie Hubbard and William Boeing in March 1919.[4] It continued as an air mail terminal with Hubbard operating a Boeing B-1 flying boat on the Victoria run, followed by others such as Vern Gorst and Percy Barnes, well into the 1930s.[5]

The hangar was sold in the 1950s and converted to a marina. You can find the location of Boeing's birthplace at the base of East Roanoke Street, off Eastlake Avenue E. It would be reasonable to expect a historical monument or even a small sign at such hallowed aviation ground, but at press time no hint can be seen of the place where Boeing began. (Rumors persist that some of the original pilings remain.) The houseboat community just north of the Roanoke Street Mini Park resides on the spot.

Birthplace of Boeing Site
East Roanoke St. and Fairview Ave. E
Seattle, WA 98102

The south end of Lake Union has been a beehive of seaplane activity from the 1920s to the present day. Early airlines such as Alaska-Washington Airways, Star Air Service, Alaska Southern, Alaska Air Transport, and Washington Aircraft and Transport opened air travel to the region. Lana Kurtzer's Flying Service provided charter air travel and flight instruction to many thousands of pilots from his Lake Union base beginning in 1931. Lake Union Air—another fixture on the lake—acquired the Kurtzer seaplane terminal after Lana Kurtzer's death in 1988. The Lake Union aviation tradition continues in the modern era with Kenmore Air (discussed further in chapter 4), whose terminal resides on the historic Kurtzer site.

Kenmore Air Lake Union Seaplane Terminal
950 Westlake Ave. N
Seattle, WA 98109
(425) 486-1257
www.kenmoreair.com

One of two Boeing B&Ws built at Boeing's Lake Union seaplane hangar, 1916.
(*The Museum of Flight Collection*)

Eddie Hubbard and Bill Boeing completed the first international air mail flight from Victoria, BC, to the Lake Union hangar in March 1919, in a Boeing Model C variant called the CL-4S. The actual mail bag in Bill Boeing's left hand is on display in the case on the left at The Museum of Flight. (*Author*)

The wonderful Museum of History and Industry (MOHAI) is close by. For devotees of Seattle area history it is a must see. It moved from its previous location in the Montlake neighborhood to the current site (former Naval and Marine Corps reserve facility) in 2012. Of special note in MOHAI's collection is their restored Boeing B-1, the oldest Boeing airplane in existence.

Museum of History and Industry (MOHAI)
860 Terry Ave. N
Seattle, WA 98109
(206) 324-1126
www.mohai.org

On the north end of the lake, one of Seattle's favorite parks, Gas Works Park, was created on the site of the Seattle Gas Light Company coal gasification plant. It offers supreme views of the sites and all the action on Lake Union. Be sure to bring your kite!

Gas Works Park
2101 N Northlake Way
Seattle, WA 98103
(206) 684-4075
http://www.seattle.gov/parks/park

Neither original B&W exists, but a replica was built in celebration of The Boeing Company's 50th anniversary in 1966. Today it can be seen hanging prominently in the Great Gallery at The Museum of Flight. (*Author*)

62

LEFT

A view of the Lake Union seaplane hangar site seen from Gas Works Park in 2014. The houseboats in the foreground float where the hangar once stood. (*Author*)

RIGHT

This small lakeside park at the base of East Roanoke Street lies just south of the site where Boeing began. The old machinery of Gas Works Park can be seen in the distance. (*Author*)

This houseboat community lies astride the site of the first Pacific Aero Products hangar and factory, the birthplace of The Boeing Company. (*Author*)

Pilot Eddie Hubbard with the Boeing B-1 mail plane at Lake Union, circa 1925. Eddie Hubbard piloted the Boeing B-1 flying boat shown here from 1920 to 1927, flying air mail on the first regularly scheduled international airmail route between Seattle and Victoria, BC. The plane could carry two passengers, plus mail and cargo.

After seven years of service without losing a single piece of mail, the B-1 was retired from airmail service in 1927. The restored plane now hangs as a featured exhibit at the Museum of History and Industry in Seattle. (*Museum of History and Industry photo and caption*)

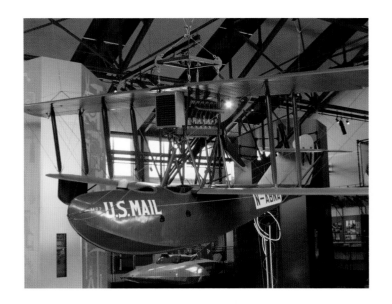

ABOVE LEFT

The Boeing B-1 (page 63) on display at the Museum of History and Industry. It is the oldest Boeing airplane in existence. (*Author*)

ABOVE RIGHT

Lockheed Vega of Alaska-Washington Airways. In addition to dozens of pioneering and record-breaking flights in the 1920s–30s, the sleek and speedy Vega was a popular airliner, as well. (*Joseph Glass Jr. Collection / The Museum of Flight*)

BELOW

The former Boeing hangar on Lake Union served as a seaplane base well into the 1950s. In this 1930s image is a Fairchild F.71, two Alaska-Washington Airways Lockheed Vegas, and a Boeing B-1E flying boat. (*The Robert W. Stevens Collection / The Museum of Flight*)

South Lake Union in the late 1940s. The USS *Rombach* (DE-364) is tied up alongside the Naval and Marine Corps Reserve training center in the foreground. The facility became the permanent home of the Museum of History and Industry in 2012. The Kurtzer Air Terminal is the white building on the left (west) shore; the site still serves seaplanes today operated by Kenmore Air. (*Museum of History and Industry*)

The old Naval Reserve Center, now the Museum of History and Industry, seen from the Kenmore Air harbor on south Lake Union in 2014. Kenmore Air de Havilland Beavers await their next journey in the foreground. (*Author*)

CHAPTER THREE

SEATTLE, WEST & DOWNTOWN

Downtown Seattle is worthy of a lengthy stay, irrespective of your passion for aviation. Great food, every coffee-based drink imaginable, world class shopping, and killer views of sea and mountains draw tourists from all over the globe. Regardless, we will keep our focus on flying history, from the earliest human flight in the region to a twenty-first century mishap.

1. Luna Park Site (Modern Anchor Park, Duwamish Head, West Seattle)
2. Boeing 307 Ditching Site (Elliott Bay)
3. Hoge Building (Bill Boeing office location)
4. Gorst Air Terminal Site (Modern Pier 54)
5. NASA Pavilion Site, 1962 World's Fair (Seattle Center)

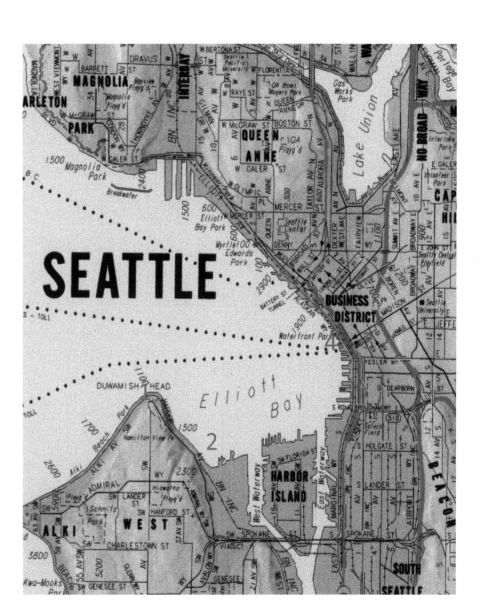

(Copyright Kroll Map Company 2015, used with permission)

WEST SEATTLE & DOWNTOWN

Little evidence in downtown Seattle suggests the city has been a plane-building capital since the early twentieth century, but before the city adopted its current official nickname of "The Emerald City" in 1982, it was commonly referred to as "Jet City" for its association with Boeing jet transports since the late 1950s. (That title has also been claimed by the city of Renton—we won't split hairs about it here.) A quick search of business names in the area turns up numerous enterprises using the "Jet City" moniker.

Long before Boeing jets, balloonists such as Park Van Tassel and L. Guy Mecklem ascended from the area in balloons and dirigibles. The first controlled human flight in the Seattle area occurred on June 27, 1908. The setting was Luna Park, a Coney Island-like amusement park that had recently opened on Duwamish Head in West Seattle. Mecklem, known as the "Wild Scotsman," set himself aloft in a dirigible of his own design. This first flight was nearly a disaster, with the gasbag rupturing. After repairs, on July 4 Mecklem raced two cars from Luna Park to the nearby Meadows complex, winning by two minutes.[1] Luna Park closed in 1913, but the outline of its natatorium (saltwater pool) forms the basis of modern Anchor Park. Historical signage pays homage to the fun-filled days when Luna Park lit up the Elliott Bay night.

Anchor Park
Near 1156 Alki Ave. SW
Seattle, WA

(While here, if you gaze upon Puget Sound to the northwest, it was from these waters that the first Boeing 314 Clipper took to the air on June 7, 1938. The crew of Eddie Allen, Earl Ferguson, and others landed on Lake Washington near Matthews Beach after a short flight.[2])

In 2002, following major restoration before flying east to the Smithsonian, the last airworthy Boeing 307 Stratoliner was forced to ditch into Elliott Bay. The crew was unhurt, the airplane was repaired, and it can now be viewed in the National Air and Space Museum Udvar-Hazy Center at Dulles Airport. The site of this mishap may be of interest not only from the historical perspective, but for its stunning Elliott Bay views—and great seafood nearby.

Boeing 307 Ditching Site
(Near Salty's on Alki Beach restaurant)
1936 Harbor Ave.
Seattle, WA
http://saltys.com/seattle

When crossing the West Seattle Bridge back toward downtown, take note of highly industrial Harbor Island to the north. Pioneering pilots in the area such as Herb Munter and Eugene Romano built and flew aircraft from this then-undeveloped area in the years prior to World War I.[3]

OPPOSITE

L. Guy Mecklem's dirigible on the boardwalk at Luna Park, likely on the date of his first test flight on June 27, 1908. This was the first human flight in the Seattle area, but following a gasbag rupture, it ended quickly with a splash in Elliott Bay. His race against two cars to The Meadows track on July 4, 1908, was much more successful and thrilled thousands of viewers. (*L. Guy Mecklem Collection Photograph 21, Center for Pacific Northwest Studies, Heritage Resources, Western Washington University*)

Luna Park, at Duwamish Head, was a popular amusement park during its short life from 1907 to 1913. The roller coaster, carousel (round, turreted building), and natatorium (far center) were among many popular attractions. Mecklem's dirigible launched from the boardwalk next to the roller coaster out of view to the right (east) of this image. (*Museum of History and Industry*)

ABOVE

Anchor Park, on Duwamish Head in West Seattle, occupies the outline of the old Luna Park natatorium. (*Author*)

ABOVE RIGHT

A diagram at Anchor Park shows the footprint of Luna Park. (*Author*)

RIGHT

The restored Boeing 307 after its deadstick ditching incident on March 28, 2002; the crew of four was unscathed. (*USCG, PA2 Sarah Foster-Snell*)

The Seattle waterfront is home to many gentrified piers, one of which was the location of Gorst Air Transport's terminal. Another operation founded by Vern Gorst of Pacific Air Transport fame, this one flew Loening Air Yachts on a cross-Sound run to/from Bremerton in the 1930s.[4] For many subsequent years the renovated pier, now Pier 54, has been home to the iconic Ivar's Acres of Clams restaurant.

Pier 54 (old Pier 3)
Ivar's Acres of Clams
1001 Alaskan Way
Seattle, WA
http://www.ivars.com/locations/acres-of-clams

An interesting, quick downtown stop for the aviation buff also interested in architecture is the Hoge Building. While his company did its work at the Duwamish (Plant 1) factory, Bill Boeing maintained an office here from the early 1920s[5] until he divested his company interests in 1934. The building was briefly Seattle's tallest in 1911, until surpassed by the nearby Smith Tower.[6] The site also happens to be the location of the first pioneer cabin in Seattle, built by Carson Boren in 1852. The Hoge Building is on the National Register of Historic Places.

Hoge Building
705 2nd Avenue (at Cherry Street)
Seattle, WA

1962 was a watershed year for Seattle and the USA in general, with the Century 21 World's Fair celebrating the dawning Space Age and the new cutting edge world of manned spaceflight. The World's Fair ran between April 21 and October 21, 1962; during that year, the first three Americans (John Glenn, Scott Carpenter, and Wally Schirra) orbited the Earth.[7] The NASA Pavilion was deservedly one of the fair's big attractions. The World's Fair site, now known as Seattle Center, is a major city gathering place for sports, concerts, and festivals. The NASA Pavilion was long ago converted to pedestrian uses, but the structures remain.

NASA Pavilion Site
Seattle Center
310 1st Ave. N
Seattle, WA

Elliott Bay and city views abound where carousels and roller coasters once thrilled Seattleites. L. Guy Mecklem piloted the first controlled flights in the area from this location. (*Author*)

LEFT

The re-restored Boeing 307 Stratoliner—none the worse for wear—at the National Air and Space Museum Udvar-Hazy Center in Virginia. It is said to be the most expensive aircraft restoration to date. (*Author*)

BELOW

The site of the Boeing 307 Stratoliner ditching in 2002, just east of Salty's on Alki Beach restaurant. (*Author*)

Six passenger Loening C-2 Air Yacht amphibians await passengers to Bremerton, circa 1933. (*Museum of History and Industry*)

ABOVE

Old Pier 3 and the Gorst Air Transport terminal site, now Pier 54 and longtime home of the beloved Ivar's Acres of Clams restaurant. (*Author*)

RIGHT

Pier 54 view from Elliott Bay in 2013. Seattle Fire Department fireboats are based just south of the pier on the site of old Grand Trunk Pacific Railway dock, which burned down in 1914. The Smith Tower rises in the background. (*Author*)

LEFT

The Hoge Building at the corner of 2nd Avenue and
Cherry Street in downtown Seattle. (*Author*)

ABOVE

The Hoge Building entrance and its more famous neighbor to
the south, the Smith Tower. Bill Boeing passed through these
doors countless times in the 1920s and '30s. (*Author*)

ABOVE LEFT

Nothing was more cutting edge at the 1962 World's Fair than the NASA Pavilion. (*Museum of History and Industry*)

ABOVE RIGHT

The NASA Pavilion building of 1962 now serves utilitarian purposes at Seattle Center. The bulk of the original building remains at its fair site at 310 1st Ave N. (*Author*)

LEFT

The east wing of the NASA Pavilion was relocated in 1995 to just south of Key Arena (Coliseum site of 1962 World's Fair) and called the Seattle Center Pavilion. The fair's icon, the Space Needle, rises above. (*Author*)

CHAPTER FOUR

SEATTLE, LAKE WASHINGTON

Lake Washington is the large body of water on the eastern shores of Seattle. Farther east lay the cities of Bellevue, Kirkland, and Redmond. At its south end is the city of Renton, which we will visit later. The lake has seen more than its share of flying history. Among notable events here, it was the beginning and end point of the first flight around the world and hosted one of the most celebrated maneuvers ever flown by a jet transport.

1. University of Washington (site of 1909 Alaska-Yukon-Pacific Exposition)

2. Sand Point Airfield / Naval Air Station Site (Magnusson Park)

3. Matthews Beach

4. Stan Sayres Memorial Park (Dash 80 Barrel Roll)

5. Kenmore Air Harbor (Kenmore)

6. Nike Missile Site S-03 (Kenmore and Lake Forest Park)

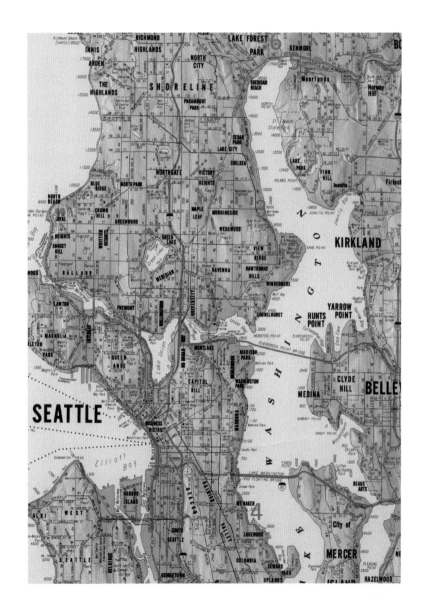

UNIVERSITY OF WASHINGTON

The present day University of Washington is the state's flagship institution of higher learning and one of the world's premier research universities. Founded in 1861, the university actually began in downtown Seattle, on the block now occupied by the Fairmont Olympic Hotel on (aptly named) University Street; it moved to the shores of Lake Washington in 1895. The site is significant for hosting the 1909 Alaska-Yukon-Pacific (A-Y-P) Exposition with its dirigible flights and for the contributions of its Department of Aeronautics & Astronautics to The Boeing Company and aviation progress in general.

The A-Y-P was held on the growing campus grounds during June 1–October 16, 1909. The grand plan of the A-Y-P fair was designed by the Olmsted brothers, whose landscape designs can be seen in cities and college campuses all over the USA.[1] It was largely retained as the UW grew rapidly in the early twentieth century: Rainier Vista and Drumheller Fountain are the most visible design elements that date to 1909. It was in this area that many thousands saw the 68-foot long dirigible operated by J. C. "Bud" Mars during the A-Y-P. These were not the first human flights in the area (those occurred by dirigible out of Luna Park as discussed in chapter 3), but the greater audience for these flights over a six-week period no doubt had larger civic impact, despite several mishaps.[2]

The UW Department of Aeronautics & Astronautics is one of the oldest such institutions. Founded in 1917 and funded largely by a wind tunnel grant from Bill Boeing, the department has produced such eminent aviation contributors as early Boeing engineer and chairman Clair Egtvedt, Boeing manufacturing genius and president Philip Johnson, World War II ace Gregory "Pappy" Boyington, crack test pilot Scott Crossfield, Gemini/Apollo astronaut Richard Gordon, 747 chief engineer Joe Sutter[3]—and your humble author—among many. Boeing's grant was not entirely altruistic—he recognized the need for a pipeline of capable engineers and his company benefited tremendously from his investment in UW Aeronautics.

In 2013, the department was formally and very appropriately named after its early patron saint, William E. Boeing.

The department is housed primarily in Guggenheim Hall, which opened in 1930 on the east side of Drumheller Fountain. Behind it is the Kirsten Wind Tunnel, named for an early giant in the department, Professor Fred Kirsten. Despite occasional threats of closure since its opening in 1938, the Kirsten Tunnel has remained in commercial operation, performing research work for academia, industry, and even bicycle racing teams. The small rectangular wind tunnel south of Kirsten is where the department began and was the first tangible evidence of Boeing's grant. Built in 1917, it is the oldest wind tunnel west of the Mississippi River and is still in use in the twenty-first century. It is now called the Aerodynamics Laboratory. The original test section hardware is now part of The Museum of Flight collection.

The "Astronautics" part of the department was added with the establishment of the Aerospace Research Lab in the early 1960s, on the south side of Guggenheim. Today it is called the Aerospace and Engineering Research Building.

While you are on campus, the old rowing shell house near Husky Stadium is worth a look. It was built by the US Navy in 1918 as a training base. The navy never used it and the storied UW rowing team was the grateful beneficiary. Now called Canoe House, it is on the National Register of Historic Places.[4] It is just south of the Waterfront Activities Center, where you can rent a canoe and explore the nearby shores.

University of Washington
Guggenheim Hall
Seattle WA 98195
206 543 9198
www.washington.edu
www.aa.washington.edu

AIRSHIP A.Y.P.E. OVER GEYSER BASIN

J. C. "Bud" Mars and his dirigible enthrall attendees of the Alaska-Yukon-Pacific Exposition in the summer of 1909. The fair's "Geyser Basin" is the site of Drumheller Fountain on the University of Washington campus today. (*University of Washington Special Collections, UW23078*)

From nearly the same spot at the University of Washington, Drumheller Fountain
(known among students as "Frosh Pond") is seen in 2012. The UW campus retained
the Olmsted A-Y-P layout in large part. (*Author*)

ABOVE

The UW "Aerodynamical Chamber" in shockingly barren surroundings shortly after its construction, around 1919. (*University of Washington Special Collections, UW 19701z*)

BELOW

The UW Aerodynamics Laboratory in 2012, still active and contributing to aeronautical knowledge and education. The author worked on a research project at this facility in the summer of 1984, adding greatly to its historical significance. (*Author*)

ABOVE

The UW Kirsten Wind Tunnel, 1939. (*University of Washington Special Collections, Todd 23048*)

BELOW

A Kirsten Wind Tunnel vignette, 2012. (*Author*)

SAND POINT AND MATTHEWS BEACH

North of the UW, Sand Point is a peninsula extending eastward into Lake Washington. Now largely Magnusson Park, the site is hugely significant in aviation as the beginning and end point of the world's first circumnavigation flight.

Sand Point Airfield began as a joint army and navy airfield in 1923. The location was chosen as the base for the army's circumnavigation flight, using four specially designed Douglas World Cruisers (DWCs). The four DWC's were numbered and named *1-Seattle, 2-Chicago, 3-Boston, 4-New Orleans*. The group departed Sand Point on April 6, 1924. *Seattle* crashed in Alaska early in the journey, and *Boston* was lost in the Atlantic on the tail end. A prototype DWC joined the army flyers for the final legs of the trip, and was christened *Boston II*. The three airplanes arrived back at Sand Point on September 28, 1924.[5] A rather humble memorial dating from the 1920s marks this event at the main entrance to Magnusson Park.

The *Chicago* can be seen at the National Air and Space Museum in Washington, DC. The *New Orleans* is on display as of this writing at the Museum of Flying, near its birthplace in Santa Monica, California. A DWC reproduction project, headed by Bob Dempster, has been ongoing in the Seattle area. The *Seattle II* made its public debut at Boeing Field in June 2013. Dempster and supporters intend to closely re-create the route of the 1924 DWC flyers and then donate the airplane to The Museum of Flight in Seattle.

Boeing aircraft were flight tested at Sand Point in the 1920s, before the advent of Gorst Field and Boeing Field.[6] The disassembly, transportation, and reassembly of airframes from the Duwamish (Plant 1) site was a major inconvenience.

A proper Naval Air Station was established at Sand Point in 1926, which remained in operation until 1970. Several of the later navy hangars are still in use for multiple purposes in the modern day Magnusson Park.

Magnusson Park
7400 Sand Point Way NE
Seattle, WA 98115

Slightly north of Sand Point we find the pleasant Matthews Beach neighborhood and park. What's the aviation connection? In 1938-39, this quiet strip of sand hosted giant Boeing 314 Clipper flying boats. Boeing used the location as a remote flight test base for the Clippers, and for a short time in 1940, Pan American Airways actually conducted Sikorsky S-42 revenue flights to Alaska from an office and dock here.[7]

Matthews Beach Park
49th Ave. NE & NE 93rd St
Seattle, WA 98118

Three of the four Douglas World Cruisers at Sand Point preparing for their world flight in March 1924. A Curtiss Jenny flies overhead. (*The Museum of Flight Collection*)

ABOVE

The Seattle World Cruiser Project headed by Bob Dempster has re-created a DWC. Here the *Seattle II* makes its public debut at The Museum of Flight in June 2013. The DWC is a large airplane. (*Courtesy of Seattle World Cruiser Association*)

BELOW

The Douglas World Cruiser *Seattle* at Sand Point. This airplane would later crash in the wilds of Alaska (its crew survived). Some of its remains can be seen today at the Alaska Aviation Heritage Museum in Anchorage. (*The Museum of Flight Collection*)

Charles Lindbergh at Sand Point, September 13, 1927, during the good will tour that followed his New York to Paris flight. (*The Museum of Flight Collection*)

88

Monument to the first world circumnavigation flight at the entrance to Magnusson Park at Sand Point, 2010. The plaque is affixed to the front of the monument. This was the former main entrance to Naval Air Station Seattle. (*Author*)

Former US Navy hangars at Sand Point, now mostly used for indoor sports. (*Author*)

The first Boeing 314 Clipper (NX-18601) in the early morning Lake Washington mist at Matthews Beach, late 1938. The airplane has its final three-tailed configuration after the initial single-tail and an experimental twin-tail proved inadequate. (*The Peter M. Bowers Collection / The Museum of Flight*)

The first three Boeing 314 Clippers at Matthews Beach, early 1939.
(*The Peter M. Bowers Collection / The Museum of Flight*)

ABOVE

A Matthews Beach panorama in 2010. In the late 1930s, Boeing 314 Clippers would dominate this view. The dock was at the right (south) end of the beach. (*Author*)

BELOW

Boeing 314 Clippers at Matthews Beach. The closest aircraft is straining at retention cables while conducting a high power engine run. (*The Peter M. Bowers Collection / The Museum of Flight*)

SEAFAIR: STAN SAYRES MEMORIAL PARK

The Boeing Model 367-80 was one of the biggest technological leaps in civil aviation. It was not the first jet transport (that honor goes to the de Havilland Comet), but it led to the wildly successful KC-135 and 707 series, which thrust The Boeing Company into a dominant industry position for decades to come. Boeing gambled with a large investment of its own money ($16 million) to launch a prototype jet transport in 1952. Better known as the "Dash 80," the swept-wing jet rolled out in May 1954, and first flew at Renton Airport on July 15, 1954.[8] Following an initial flight test program, the airplane was used on demonstration flights for marketing to airlines.

One of the highlights of Seattle's short summer season each year is the civic festival known as "Seafair." The culminating event of Seafair is the unlimited hydroplane race on Lake Washington during the first weekend of August. Several hundred thousand people flock to the shores to see the spectacle—still the largest single sporting event in the region well into the twenty-first century.

The hydroplane course is set up between the I-90 bridge to the north and Seward Park to the south, adjacent to Seattle's Mount Baker neighborhood. The nerve center of this uniquely Seattle event is the hydroplane pits that take over Stan Sayres Memorial Park (itself named for one of the pioneers of the sport). Grand views of the hydroplane course area can be had here and all along Lake Washington Boulevard in the neighborhood.

Stan Sayres Park
3808 Lake Washington Blvd. S
Seattle, WA 98118

In addition to his later flying exploits and executive career, legendary Boeing test pilot Brien Wygle was also a top hydroplane driver during the late 1950s and raced on these waters.

A hugely popular tradition of the Seafair hydroplane races is the airshow highlighted by the US Navy Blue Angels. Since the 1950s, the "Blues" have performed every year over Lake Washington—with a few exceptions for political or other reasons.

On August 6, 1955, Seafair hosted the Gold Cup race, and in addition to the usual throngs, Boeing President Bill Allen hosted a gathering of airline and industry leaders. Rather than the planned simple fly-by of the new Dash 80, Boeing test pilot "Tex" Johnston pulled the brown and yellow bird into a barrel roll. Although the maneuver when properly flown is relatively benign, it looks spectacular and is exceedingly rare for a big jet. With the crowd buzzing, Johnston swung around for a second pass and did it again![9] Although Allen subsequently chastised Johnston for the unauthorized maneuver, there is little doubt of the impression it left on airline executives and the public.

Not frequently mentioned is the rest of the Dash 80's flight crew that day: co-pilot Jim Gannett and flight engineer Dix Loesch.[10] There was at least one fellow with a camera in the back…

The Dash 80 had a later extensive career as a technology testbed, including aerial refueling, high lift devices, propulsion systems, and fly-by-wire control systems before being retired to the desert in 1972. In the 1990s, it was ferried to Seattle for restoration and flew to its permanent home in 2003. The Dash 80—one of the true icons of American aviation—can be seen today in the National Air and Space Museum Udvar-Hazy Center at Dulles Airport in Virginia.

Everyone has enjoyed gazing at the scenery that unfolds from an airliner window; rarely does it look like this! This remarkable view over the starboard wing of the Dash 80 was taken during the first of two barrel rolls on August 6, 1955. It shows downtown Seattle at center left and the edge of Lake Washington at upper right. Sharp-eyed observers will note the Smith Tower visible on the left among the row of Seattle piers. At lower left is Duwamish Head, site of the old Luna Park and the first dirigible flights in the region. This famous photo was taken by test engineer Bell Whitehead from the forward cabin and is shown the way he saw the scene. If you find it disorienting, simply make like Tex Johnston and roll the book! (*Copyright © Boeing – used with permission*)

ABOVE

This Boeing 737 is departing Sea-Tac airport on a line roughly parallel to that flown by the Dash 80 at the Seafair Gold Cup in 1955. The Seafair hydroplane course, essentially unchanged since its beginning in 1950, is set up temporarily each August south of the Interstate 90 bridge at center and north of the Seward Park peninsula on the right. (*Author*)

RIGHT

The pier at Stan Sayres Park on Lake Washington, ground zero for hydroplane racing during Seafair week in early August each year. Tex Johnston and the Dash 80 crew flew their famous barrel rolls in these blue skies. (*Author*)

ABOVE LEFT

After years in desert storage, the Dash 80 underwent extensive restoration in Seattle. Approximately forty-eight years after its famous Seafair barrel rolls, the Dash 80 departed Boeing Field for the final time on August 24, 2003. (*Author*)

LEFT

The Dash 80 lies beyond the Boeing 307 Stratoliner in a well-deserved place of honor at the National Air and Space Museum Udvar-Hazy Center, Virginia. (*Author*)

ABOVE RIGHT

The Blue Angels make a delta formation pass at Seafair in 1986. This was the final year the team flew the McDonnell-Douglas A-4 Skyhawk. (*Author*)

KENMORE

At the north end of Lake Washington, the town of Kenmore is host to an airline still operating in the same spirit as pioneering 1930s carriers such as Alaska-Washington Airways. Kenmore Air was founded in 1946 and has operated from its namesake base ever since. They are among the world's premier seaplane operations, flying de Havilland Beavers & Otters, Cessna Caravans and 180s, and other types to destinations in Washington and British Columbia.[11] They also operate from the historic South Lake Union base in Seattle. Kenmore Air is a true slice of living aviation history, and they would be happy to whisk you to the San Juan Islands, Victoria, BC, or beyond.

Kenmore Air Harbor
6321 NE 175th St.
Kenmore, WA 98028
425-486-1257
www.kenmoreair.com

During the perilous early years of the Cold War, the skies over the Pacific Northwest were protected by a ring of US Army Nike anti-aircraft missile sites. In addition to large metropolitan areas such as Seattle and Tacoma, the state's major military installations needed protection from the threat of nuclear attack via long-range Soviet bombers.

The first US Army Nike Ajax missiles arrived in the area in 1954. With overall Seattle Defense Area control based at Ft. Lawton in north Seattle, launch sites sprang up all over the Puget Sound, including Kenmore (S-03), Redmond (S-13/S-14, a double site), Kent (S-43/S-45, another double site), Kingston (S-92, on the Kitsap Peninsula), and other locations. Other Nike networks defended eastern Washington. In the late 1950s, the more effective Nike

Hercules missile began to replace the Ajax, resulting in some sites closing. By 1974, all Nike sites in Washington were dismantled. They have gradually been converted into government offices, parks, or sold to private interests. None of the sites in the area are intact, and frankly very little remains to be seen. The endnotes provide further details for researching individual sites.[12]

The S-03 site in Kenmore is representative of these facilities and their transformation over time; the control and administration center is now Horizon View Park and the launch center (approximately two miles away) is now a Federal Emergency Management Agency (FEMA) facility and Army Reserve Center.

Former Kenmore Nike Missile Site (S-03)
Control/Admin Ctr
47th Ave. NE (south of 201st St) (Horizon View Park)
Lake Forest Park, WA 98155

Launch Site
130 228th St. SW (FEMA Regional Headquarters /
   Army Reserve Center)
Bothell, WA 98021

LEFT

Kenmore Air Harbor in 1952. In addition to the fleet of Taylorcraft and Aeronca floatplanes ready for passengers, the back ramp is full of Republic Seabees. Kenmore was the northwest regional Seabee dealer at this time. Three Norduyn Norsemen can also be seen on the right. (*Courtesy of Kenmore Air Harbor, Inc.*)

BELOW LEFT

Two de Havilland turbine Otters at the busy Kenmore Air Harbor at the north end of Lake Washington, 2013. (*Author*)

BELOW RIGHT

Kenmore Air purchased Edo Floats in 1998, and provides Edo service for their own fleet and customers worldwide. (*Author*)

Nike-Ajax missile battery at Redmond, WA, July 1955.
Other Puget Sound Nike sites were similar. (*Eastside Heritage Center*)

ABOVE LEFT

Interpretive sign at the control and administration center for the Nike S-03 site. This area is now Horizon View Park in Lake Forest Park, WA. (*Author*)

ABOVE RIGHT

The former launch site for Nike site S-03 (Kenmore), now a FEMA and Army Reserve facility. (*Author*)

LEFT

The remains of a Nike S-03 site radar pad at Horizon View Park.

CHAPTER FIVE

SOUTH KING COUNTY & TACOMA

The southern region of greater Seattle includes aviation sites of distant historical interest as well as vital modern functions. Lying between Seattle and Tacoma is the region's major commercial airport, aptly named "Sea-Tac." To the east, in the Kent Valley, is one of the region's first (and long gone) air fields and a Boeing facility where cutting edge spacecraft were born. Farther south, beyond Tacoma, is Joint Base Lewis-McChord, a very active US Army and Air Force installation with aviation roots in the 1920s.

1. Seattle-Tacoma International Airport

2. Munter Field Site, Kent

3. Boeing Kent Space Center

4. Mueller-Harkins Field Site (Clover Park Technical College)

5. McChord Field (Joint Base Lewis-McChord), Tacoma

6. Gray Army Air Field (former Camp Lewis, Joint Base Lewis-McChord, Tacoma - slightly farther south than shown)

(Copyright Kroll Map Company 2015, used with permission)

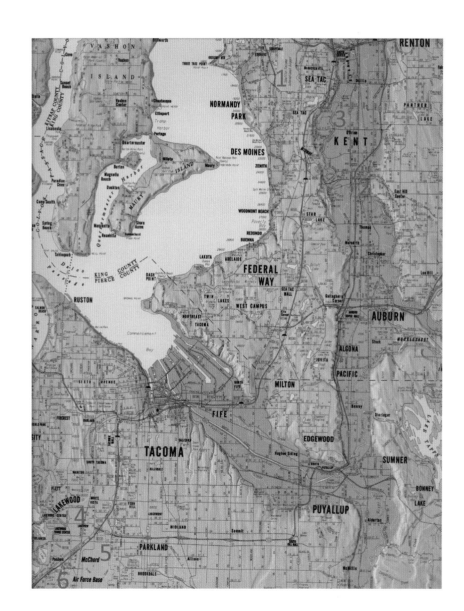

SEA-TAC AND KENT

Seattle-Tacoma International Airport (SEA), better known as "Sea-Tac," was established during World War II. Originally known as Bow Lake Airport, its purpose was civil, to offload nearby Boeing Field for military duties.[1] The central terminal has expanded over the years to include concourses A through D during the 1960s and '70s. North and South satellite terminals and large parking garages were added in the 1970s. Remodeling and expansion continue to serve the area's growing air traffic. The original runways gave way to today's runway 16L/34R, which was lengthened for jets in 1959–61.[2] A second runway was later added, and finally a third runway was completed (a Herculean project) in 2008, to allow simultaneous instrument landing system (ILS) approaches.

In the late 1940s, Northwest and United Airlines were the pioneer operators at Sea-Tac, with Western, Alaska, and Pan Am joining soon. Scandinavian Airways System (SAS) inaugurated DC-8 jet service with their route to Copenhagen in 1966.[3] Perhaps the most notorious event associated with the airport was the November 1971 highjacking of Northwest Flight 305 by D. B. Cooper—despite tantalizing clues over the years, his parachute jump and disappearance remains a mystery.[4] Seattle has served as headquarters of Alaska Airlines since 1953, whose many Boeing 737s with the Eskimo tail are ubiquitous at Sea-Tac.

Sea-Tac Airport
1701 International Blvd.
Seattle, WA 98158
(206) 787-5388
www.portseattle.org/sea-tac

Nearby Kent Valley saw everything from Curtiss Jennies to advanced spacecraft during the twentieth century. Before there was Boeing Field, Herb Munter established an airfield in a Green River valley cow pasture a few miles south. Munter was one of the first pilots in the Northwest and served as a test pilot for Bill Boeing's new company in its early years. Munter flew charter and photography flights from this location in the early 1920s, including the first ever flight over Mt. Rainier in a custom built Boeing BB-L6 on May 24, 1920.[5] Originally known as Munter Field, Munter's association with the facility and aviation in general appear to have ended after a fire destroyed hangars and several aircraft in the mid-1920s. Jennies returned to the location with the Becvar Brothers' Kent Flying Service, but by 1931, aviation activities here succumbed to the Great Depression and the cows returned.[6] In modern times, the site is mostly occupied by the A-1 Pallets company. No aviation traces remain.

Munter Field Site
A-1 Pallets
S 259th St. and 3rd Ave. S
Kent, WA 98032
www.a1palletcompany.com

(Another Kent general aviation airport about a half mile south of the Munter Field site was in operation during the 1940s through the 1960s. By the mid-1970s, it was redeveloped and no evidence of its existence can now be seen.[7]) Further south in the city of Auburn, Boeing's Fabrication Division was established in 1965 to support the needs of the company's programs. Long tractor trailer rigs carrying Auburn wing spars to Renton and Everett are a common site on area freeways. The author's children were often thrilled to wave at the low-riding rear axle drivers of these trucks.

The passenger terminal on Seattle-Tacoma Airport Terminal opening day, July 9, 1949. Port of Seattle officials estimated that 30,000 people attended the opening to tour the new airport and inspect several aircraft, including a Northwest Boeing 377 making its debut, a Pan American DC-4, and an Air Force C-82 Packet (presumably from nearby McChord Field). A B-17 is also visible on the far left. The then state-of-the-art 377 Stratocruiser seems to be attracting most of the attention. The original parking lot was replaced with a parking garage in the 1970s, significantly expanded in the 1990s. (*Museum of History and Industry*)

ABOVE

The much-remodeled central terminal at Sea-Tac, with Mt. Rainier on the horizon in 2014. The original control tower seen here was supplanted by an all-new stand-alone tower to the north in 2004. (*Author*)

BELOW

Alaska Airlines 737s are nearly synonymous with modern Sea-Tac. (*Author*)

A couple of Sea-Tac accidents…

ALASKA AIRLINES FLIGHT 009, DOUGLAS C-54, SEA-TAC AIRPORT, NOVEMBER 30, 1947
A too long and too fast landing in poor weather resulted in an overrun of this C-54 (variant of the DC-4). The Civil Aeronautics Board report[8] summarized the accident:

At 1425, November 30, 1947, Alaska Airlines' non-scheduled Flight 009, a C-54 airplane, NC-91009, went off the end of a wet runway at the Seattle-Tacoma Airport, Seattle, Washington, and collided with a moving automobile. Eight of the 28 occupants of the aircraft and one occupant of the automobile were killed. Seventeen occupants of the aircraft suffered injuries. The aircraft was destroyed.

Aerial view appearing to be from a Curtiss Jenny of Munter Field in Kent in the late 1920s. Scenic Hill rises in the background. (*The Museum of Flight Collection*)

The airplane "went off the end of the runway, crossed 229 feet of wet ground, and then rolled down a 24-foot embankment. At the bottom of the embankment it struck a ditch which sheared off the left lending gear and the left wing. The aircraft continued on to the intersection of the Des Moines Highway and South 188th Street where it collided with a moving automobile. Spilled gasoline was ignited, and the wreckage was enveloped in flames." There is no trace of the accident to be seen today.

South 188th St.
Near Sea-Tac Runway 16L/34R overpass
Seatac, WA

NORTHWEST ORIENT FLIGHT 2, BOEING 377, NEAR MAURY ISLAND, WA, APRIL 2 1956

The Boeing 377 was a commercial derivative of the B-29 bomber and one of the premier airliners of the early 1950s. A flight engineer error mismanaging engine cowl flaps for takeoff led to the loss of this Stratocruiser that ditched into Puget Sound. The Civil Aeronautics Board report[9] summarized the accident:

Northwest Airlines Flight 2, a B-377, N 74608, was ditched in Puget Sound, 4.7 nautical miles southwest of Seattle-Tacoma Airport, April 2, 1956, at 0810, approximately four minutes after takeoff. All occupants successfully evacuated the aircraft but four of the 32 passengers and one of the crew of six drowned. Two passengers incurred minor injuries during the ditching. The aircraft, although later recovered, was a total loss.

The airplane's watery crash site was just east of Point Robinson Lighthouse on Maury Island (connected to Vashon Island). It was quickly salvaged.[10]

Point Robinson Lighthouse
3705 SW Point Robinson Rd.
Vashon, WA

Although there are larger and more famous Boeing facilities in the Seattle area, none can claim to surpass the innovative machines that have emerged from the Kent Space Center in the Green River Valley. Opening in 1964, such products as the Lunar Orbiter, Lunar Roving Vehicle, Air Launched Cruise Missile, and Inertial Upper Stage were largely designed and/or produced here.[11] Boeing has been selling off major elements of this property since the mid-2000s. Little can be seen except for building exteriors from a distance, and these appear subject to an accelerating pace of demolition as the site is redeveloped. The best views are from West Valley Highway on the east side and along Frager Road on the west side. There is no public access.

Boeing Kent Space Center
West Valley Highway and S 212th St.
Kent, WA

Site of Munter Field on the south side of Kent from South 259th St. in 2013, now home of A-1 Pallets. (*Author*)

ABOVE

Aerial view of Kent Space Center, mid-1980s. (*Copyright © Boeing – used with permission*)

BELOW

Boeing Kent Space Center and Green River from Frager Road in 2012. (*Author*)

TACOMA AREA

Rudy Mueller and Leo Harkins acquired the Tacoma Speedway—a popular automobile racetrack—in 1922; they established a private airfield and flying service at the site. Vern Gorst's Pacific Air Transport began airmail service here in September 1927. Tacoma Flying Service and others conducted pilot training at the airfield in the early 1940s. The airport closed in 1944 and became a naval supply depot. In 1949, the navy surplused the site and it was acquired by the Clover Park School District, eventually becoming Clover Park Technical College. In the early 1970s, the school resumed airport operations until the strip was closed for good in 2001.[12] The school's Building 5 in the northeast corner of the campus is the old Mueller-Harkins hangar with a commemorative plaque on the west wall.

Clover Park Technical College
4500 Steilacoom Blvd. SW
Lakewood, WA 98499

Today's McChord Field at Joint Base Lewis-McChord (JBLM) had its origins as a civil airfield, christened Tacoma Field in 1929. The facility was briefly known as Pierce County Airport, and was chosen as a military site in support of the nearby and massive Fort Lewis. Transferred to the US government in 1938, it was renamed for Col. William McChord, a fallen Army Air Corps aviator.[13]

The history of the field—later to become McChord Air Force Base—is much too lengthy for recounting here. The base has primarily hosted airlift and interceptor units. Its runways have seen dozens of aircraft types, from B-18 Bolos to transports such as the C-82 Packet, C-124 Globemaster, C-141 Starlifter, and C-17. Interceptors have run the gamut from P-38 Lightnings, P-61 Black Widows, and F-82 Twin Mustangs to F-86 Sabres, F-102 Delta Daggers, F-106 Delta Darts, and F-15 Eagles.[14] The Northwest air defense mission was transitioned to the Oregon Air National Guard, operating out of Portland International Airport, in 1989.

Today, McChord Field hosts the C-17 Globemaster IIIs of the 62nd Airlift Wing. At the time of this writing, the McChord Air Museum is open to the public, but check their website for latest information. There is both a small indoor museum and an outdoor air park overlooking the main runway. The air park is notable for displaying well preserved examples of most of the significant aircraft types to serve at the base.

McChord Field Visitor Center
Joint Base Lewis-McChord
(253) 982-2119
www.mcchordairmuseum.org

OPPOSITE

On September 7, 1927, direct airmail and passenger service was inaugurated at Tacoma's Mueller-Harkins airport. After the first bag of airmail arrived, Postmaster Clyde J. Backus (right) turned it over to department employee Alfred Bottiger (left), who carried it to the city by automobile. Pictured in the center is Rudy Mueller. Over 2,500 people waited two hours at the airport to cheer the arrival of the first airmail plane of the Pacific Air Transport Co. (*Photo and caption Tacoma Public Library, G12.1-080*)

In February 1940, the Tacoma Flying Service was one of three aeronautical firms with headquarters at Mueller-Harkins Airport. (*Tacoma Public Library, A9405-5*)

The army side of JBLM Fort Lewis is the site of one of the earliest airfields in the region, with flying activity as early as 1921. Then Camp Lewis, it was named for Meriwether Lewis of the Lewis and Clark Expedition. A highlight of the early years was two visits of the giant US Navy airship *Shenandoah* in 1924. The airfield was named for Capt. Lawrence Gray, a fallen army dirigible balloonist, in 1938. Gray Army Airfield (GAAF) hosted observation units during World War II and played a leading role in helicopter airmobility and anti-tank weapon development during the Vietnam War. In later years it was a center for testing the UH-60 Blackhawk and was home to mountain rescue units flying the CH-47 Chinook.[15] In the twenty-first century it is home to the rotary winged assets of a special operations battalion, an aviation brigade, and the Washington Air National Guard.

There is no public access to GAAF, but visitors may learn about the history of Fort Lewis at the nearby Lewis Army Museum. Hours are limited and a base pass must be obtained to visit; check the museum website for current information.

Lewis Army Museum
Constitution Drive
Joint Base Lewis-McChord, WA 98433
(253) 967-7206
www.lewis-mcchord.army.mil/dptms/museum/museum.htm
www.fortlewismuseum.com

LEFT

The Mueller-Harkins hangar in 2015, now Building 5 at Clover Park Technical College. A commemorative plaque is installed on the wall to the right of the right hand door. (*Author*)

BELOW

On July 28, 1929, Harold Bromley intended to be the first pilot to fly solo and nonstop across the Pacific. The flight launched from Tacoma Field, an area that is now part of the McChord Field complex. The first *City of Tacoma* (a Lockheed Explorer) is poised at the top of a ramp designed to assist takeoff performance. It crashed on takeoff, but Bromley survived and went on to a long flying career, including further unsuccessful attempts to fly to Tokyo. (*Tacoma Public Library, G12.1-094D*)

On July 3, 1940, as part of the dedication ceremony and air show at McChord Field, an early model B-17 Flying Fortress used three of its engines to maneuver on the runway. Approximately 10,000 visitors swarmed over the US Army's newest airbase to see the $6 million facility. Hangar 3 is visible in the background. (*Photo and caption Tacoma Public Library, D9973-4*)

A flotilla of Douglas B-18 bombers grace the ramp adjacent to Hangars 1 and 2, June 1940. The "BQ" designation on the tails indicates aircraft of the 17th Bombardment Group. Note the visiting US Army Air Corps Northrop A-17 on the left. (*Tacoma Public Library, D9918-7*)

ABOVE

Two of the first types to serve at McChord—the Douglas B-18A Bolo (left) and Douglas B-23 Dragon (tail at right)—at the McChord Air Museum air park. (*Author*)

ABOVE RIGHT

The Lockheed C-141 Starlifter was an iconic presence at McChord from the 1960s until being displaced by the McDonnell-Douglas C-17 in the 1990s. (*Author*)

BELOW

The 318th Fighter Interceptor Squadron and their signature star insignia guarded northwest skies from 1942 to 1989. This Convair F-106 Delta Dart bears the name of Capt. Randy Neville, who would fly on the first flight of the Boeing 787 in December 2009. (*Author*)

The US Navy dirigible *Shenandoah* mooring at Camp Lewis in October 1924. A 165-foot tall mooring mast was specially constructed for the visit. The giant dirigible was patterned after a German zeppelin captured by the French in 1917. On September 3, 1925, the airship was destroyed in a thunderstorm over Noble County, Ohio, taking the lives of fourteen of its forty-three crew members. The mast, apparently northeast of today's Gray Army Air Field, was dismantled in 1936. (*Tacoma Public Library, C162610-5*)

CHAPTER SIX

RENTON

The city of Renton is home to a historic World War II facility that became the most productive jet factory on Earth. It was also the jump-off point of the ill-fated journey of Wiley Post and Will Rogers to Alaska in 1935.

1. Renton Municipal Airport (Clayton Scott Field)
2. Will Rogers-Wiley Post Memorial Seaplane Base, Bryn Mawr
3. Boeing Renton Plant

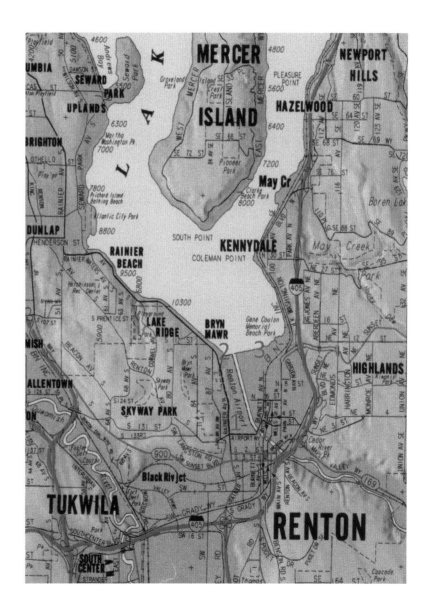

(Copyright Kroll Map Company 2015, used with permission)

RENTON AIRPORT AREA

In the 1930s, the Bryn Mawr seaplane base was the aviation hub of south Lake Washington. Wiley Post's hybrid Lockheed Orion-Explorer airplane received its floats here before heading north to Alaska and destiny. Post and humorist Will Rogers perished when the airplane crashed near Barrow on August 15, 1935.[1]

Renton Municipal Airport (RNT) rose from the wetlands at the south end of Lake Washington along with the Boeing factory during World War II. Renton Field was officially renamed Clayton Scott Field in 2005.

Clayton Scott Field
616 Perimeter Rd. W
Renton, WA 98057
(425) 420-7471

The Boeing Renton plant began as a US Navy facility intended for production of the Boeing Sea Ranger flying boat during the war[2]; that project was soon displaced by the urgent need to build the B-29 Superfortress. After the war, Renton produced the Boeing C-97, 707/KC-135, 727, 737 series in its many forms, and the 757. Boeing even manufactured military and civilian hydrofoil boats here in the 1970s.

Many thousands of Boeing aircraft have taken wing from the company's Renton plant and adjacent Renton Airport. In modern times, rarely a day goes by without a new 737 making its first flight. The first 737s were built at Plant 2 and the Thompson Site at Boeing Field, but production moved to Renton in 1970. Fuselage sections are assembled in Wichita, Kansas, and shipped by rail to Renton for final assembly.

No public tours of the Boeing Renton plant are available, but several locations offer excellent views of the airport and production activity:

Clayton Scott Memorial (south perimeter, off Airport Way)

Chamber of Commerce overlook (southwest corner, off Rainier Ave. S)

Will Rogers / Wiley Post Memorial Seaplane Base (northwest corner, W Perimeter Rd., access via Rainier Ave. S)

Cedar River Trail, 600 Nishiwaki Lane (take Logan Ave. N to N 6th St., proceed west to Nishiwaki Lane)

Gene Coulon Memorial Beach Park, 1201 Lake Washington Boulevard North

The shopping area known as The Landing, off I-405 exit 5, also provides multiple views of the Boeing Renton plant.

Renton also happens to be home to the NFL's Seattle Seahawks, whose headquarters and practice facility is just northeast of Renton Airport.

OPPOSITE

Humorist Will Rogers and aviation pioneer Wiley Post pose on August 7, 1935, at Renton Field, shortly before leaving on their ill-fated journey. The two men planned to explore a new route to Europe over Alaska and Siberia in the modified Lockheed Orion-Explorer. Northwest Air Service in Renton installed the large floats to enable landings in Alaska and Siberia. The expedition ended when the plane crashed outside Point Barrow, Alaska, on August 15, killing both men. Small components of this aircraft survive in The Museum of Flight Collection. (*Museum of History and Industry*)

Technicians at Renton Field work on Wiley Post's airplane in August 1935. It was a hybrid with a Lockheed Orion fuselage and Lockheed Explorer wings equipped with a 550 HP Wasp engine and oversize 260-gallon gas tanks. The large floats were installed by Northwest Air Service at Bryn Mawr, in Renton. (*Museum of History and Industry*)

LEFT

Monument to Will Rogers and Wiley Post at the small park and seaplane base named for the famous duo at the old Bryn Mawr site on the north end of Renton Field. Seaplane operations have continued at this location since the 1930s. (*Author*)

BELOW

Boeing B-29 assembly line in Renton, March 1945. This was the first major role for the Renton factory. The open door in the distance faces Lake Washington. (*The Boeing Company Collection at The Museum of Flight*)

Boeing B-29 Superfortress in flight over the Cascade Mountains of Washington, circa 1944. The B-29 was the most technologically advanced airplane produced during World War II, including guns that could be fired by remote control. The crew areas were pressurized and connected by a long tube through the bomb bays. Modifications led to the B-29D, upgraded to the B-50, and the RB-29 photo reconnaissance aircraft. A total of 3,970 B-29s were built, 1,119 of those at Renton. (*Copyright © Boeing, used with permission*)

LEFT

Clayton Scott Memorial, at the south end of Renton Airport. Scott had a long and distinguished flying career in the northwest, including the novelty of being the first pilot to land and take off from the nearby strip that would become Boeing Field. He flew for Gorst Air Transport, was Bill Boeing's personal pilot in the 1930s, and was chief production test pilot at Boeing from 1940 to 1966. He passed away in 2006 at the age of 101. (*Author*)

BELOW

The Boeing Renton plant in the 1960s, at Renton Municipal Airport on the south shore of Lake Washington. Two newly assembled 707s sit on the tarmac adjacent to Bldg. 4-20 at center, the oldest part of the plant. A collection of 707s, 727s, and 737s await paint and production flight test on the far end of runway 15/33 (renamed 16/34 in 2009). The floating lumber on the lake is associated with the old Barbee Mill that closed in 2002. The Bryn Mawr seaplane base site, now renamed for Will Rogers and Wiley Post, is in the area just off the lower right edge of the photo. (*The Museum of Flight Collection*)

124

SIGNIFICANT FIRST FLIGHTS AT RENTON FIELD[3]

Boeing Model 367-80 "Dash 80," 707 Prototype (July 15, 1954), Tex Johnston and Dix Loesch

Boeing 727 (February 9, 1963), Lew Wallick, Dix Loesch, and M. K. Schuelenberger

Boeing 757 (February 19, 1982), John Armstrong and Lew Wallick

ABOVE

The oldest part of the Boeing Renton plant, Building 4-20 with its signature sawtooth roofline is easily visible from the Cedar River Trail on the east side of Renton Airport. (*Author*)

LEFT

Green 737s on rails are a common site in Renton, arriving from Wichita for final assembly. The green color is associated with protective material applied until the aircraft are painted. (*Courtesy of Jim Schubert*)

CHAPTER SEVEN

EVERETT

The area surrounding the Snohomish County Airport— more commonly known as Paine Field—represents an embarrassment of riches for the aviation enthusiast. Major air museums and collections dot each quadrant of the facility, with the largest airplane factory (and building) in the world on one end.

1. Paine Field

2. Boeing Everett Plant

3. Future of Flight & Boeing Tour

4. The Museum of Flight Restoration Center and Reserve Collection

5. Flying Heritage Collection

6. Historic Flight Foundation

7. Legend Flyers (former Me-262 Project)

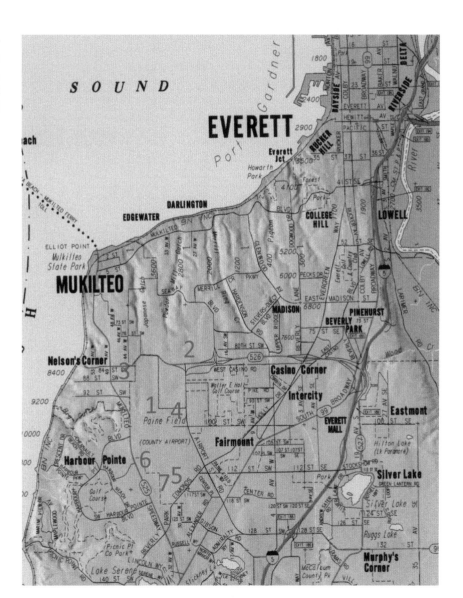

PAINE FIELD

Snohomish County Airport in south Everett, better known as Paine Field (PAE), was built during the mid-1930s, during the depths of the Great Depression. Primarily used by the army and later Air Force Air Defense Command, everything changed when Boeing selected a site on the northeast corner of the facility in 1966 to build the 747 jumbo jet.[1] Continually expanded since then, the Boeing Everett factory is the largest building in the world by volume. The latest addition is the 777X composite wing center, which began construction in 2014.

Paine Field was named for Topliff Paine (1893–1922), a World War I and mailplane pilot hailing from Everett.[2]

Since 1969, Paine Field has hosted the first flights of all major Boeing wide-body types: the 747 (1969), 767 (1981), 777 (1994), and 787 (2009). With the exception of some 787s being built in South Carolina, every production article of these aircraft types has been delivered from Paine.

Paine Field hosted popular air shows from 1946 onward. From 1969 to 1992, the Lynnwood Rotary Club sponsored the state's largest air show. The USAF Thunderbirds, US Navy Blue Angels, and RCAF Snowbirds all performed here. Pilot extraordinaire Bob Hoover, exotic Soviet types such as the Su-27 Flanker and massive six-engined An-225, and locally stationed US Army Reserve CH-47 Chinook helicopters also graced these skies.[3]

In the twenty-first century, in addition to Boeing test and delivery flights, Paine is a vibrant, working airport. It is ringed with general aviation facilities, suppliers, aircraft modification centers, flight schools, and museums galore.

The Bomarc Business Park, at 2600 94th St. SW on the east side of Paine Field, stands on the grounds of a planned Bomarc missile site. (The Bomarc was a surface to air missile designed to counter the Soviet bomber menace during the Cold War.) The project was abandoned in the early 1960s when the missile became obsolete and the site never became operational.

Plan for a long, busy, and very enjoyable day visiting Paine Field and its attractions. You really need two days to do it justice.

Paine Field Airport Administration
3220 110th St. SW
Everett WA 98204
425 388 5125
www.painefield.com

ABOVE

747 #1 (RA001) takes wing for the first time on February 9, 1969. If there is a single icon of air travel in the last fifty years, the Boeing 747 is it. (*The Boeing Company Collection at The Museum of Flight*)

RIGHT

747 RA001 at The Museum of Flight following its restoration to beautiful condition in 2014. (*Author*)

RIGHT

The Boeing Everett plant in the early 1970s, and a flight line full of early 747s. Gardner Bay, the city of Everett, and Mt. Baker lie to the north. The factory was expanded eastward (to the right in the photo) in the late 1970s for the 767 program and again in the early 1990s for the 777. The 787 production line made use of existing space in the mid-2000s. (*The Museum of Flight Collection*)

BELOW

Paine Field runway 16R/34L, the Boeing Everett factory, and the flight line looking southeast from the Future of Flight Strato Deck. A mix of 777s, 787s, 747-8s, and a KC-46 tanker await delivery in the summer of 2015. (*Author*)

OPPOSITE

Boeing 787 #1 (ZA001) takes to the sky for the first time from KPAE 34L on December 15, 2009. (*Author*)

SIGNIFICANT FIRST FLIGHTS AT PAINE FIELD[4]

Boeing 747 (February 9, 1969), Jack Waddell, Brien Wygle, and Jessie Wallick

Boeing 767 (September 26, 1981), Tom Edmonds, Lew Wallick, and John Britt

Boeing 777 (June 12, 1994), John Cashman and Ken Higgins

Boeing 787 (December 15, 2009), Mike Carriker and Randy Neville

AROUND PAINE FIELD

While at Paine Field you *must* see:

Flying Heritage Collection
3407 109th St. SW
Everett, WA 98204
(877) 342-3404
www.flyingheritage.com

Paul Allen's magnificent collection of (mostly) WWII warbirds is perhaps the finest collection of authentically restored, airworthy examples of these types in the world. View the collection and in the summer watch them fly (check website for schedule).

Future of Flight
(Aviation Center & Boeing Tour)
8415 Paine Field Blvd.
Mukilteo, WA 98275
(800) 464-1476
www.futureofflight.org

Rather than the usual historical focus of museums, FoF concentrates on the cutting edge technology that will shape aircraft of tomorrow. It is also home base for the Boeing Everett factory tour.

Historic Flight Foundation
10719 Bernie Webber Dr.
Mukilteo, WA 98275
(425) 348-3200
www.historicflight.org

The airworthy collection of John Sessions is more eclectic than Flying Heritage, but no less impressive. This is perhaps the most accessible assemblage of vintage aircraft in the Northwest. The enthusiastic Mr. Sessions flies them all and is often on site, happy to share information and experiences.

Legend Flyers (Me-262 Project)
10728 36th Place West
Building 221, Bay 3
Everett, WA 98204
(425) 290-7878
www.stormbirds.com/project/index.html

This restoration organization has reproduced several Messerschmitt Me-262 aircraft and continues with other projects. Tours and hours are limited—please check in advance.

**The Museum of Flight Restoration Center
and Reserve Collection**
2909 100th St. SW
Everett, WA 98204
(206) 764-5720
www.museumofflight.org

The main museum campus is at Boeing Field (see chapter 1), but this facility is where the serious work of aircraft restoration takes place. The friendly staff will gladly show you around.

Alaska Airlines operated a maintenance facility on the south end of Paine Field in the 1950s. Here Alaska DC-4s and C-46s undergo heavy checks. (*Used by permission, The Daily Herald, Everett, WA via Everett Public Library*)

The same hangar today is home to the fabulous Flying Heritage Collection. (*Courtesy of FHC and Owen Richards*)

CHAPTER EIGHT

BEYOND

Seattle does not have a monopoly on major aviation history in the Pacific Northwest; venturing beyond the Jet City metropolis will offer rich rewards for the aviation enthusiast. Awaiting you are the landing sites of epic oceanic crossings, a daredevil's rooftop, and much more.

1. Fancher Field Site (East Wenatchee, WA)
2. Pearson Field (Vancouver, WA)
3. Multnomah Hotel Site (Embassy Suites, Portland, OR)
4. Boeing 307 Crash Site (1939) (near Alder, WA)
5. Boeing 707 Crash Site (1959) (near Oso, WA)
6. Arlington Airport
7. Naval Air Station Whidbey Island (Oak Harbor, WA)
8. Bellevue Airport Site
9. Issaquah Airport Site
10. Grant County Airport (Moses Lake, WA)
11. Felts Field (Spokane, WA)
12. Fairchild Air Force Base (Spokane, WA)

(Not shown - Medford Airport, Medford, OR)

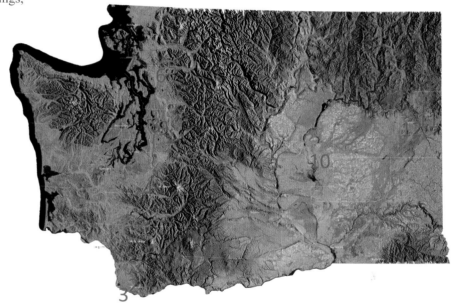

(*US Geological Survey*)

FANCHER FIELD, EAST WENATCHEE, WA

One of the most impressive aviation firsts that almost no one knows about ended on the heights above the Columbia River in East Wenatchee. On October 4–5, 1931, Clyde Pangborn and Hugh Herndon flew a highly modified Bellanca J-300 named *Miss Veedol* from Misawa, Japan, to East Wenatchee—the first non-stop flight across the vast Pacific Ocean.[1] To save fuel, the landing gear was modified to be jettisoned after takeoff; when the gear did not separate cleanly Pangborn had to exit the cabin to force them to fall away.

Bad weather in the Pacific Northwest caused the duo to consider landing at, in turn, Boise, Spokane, and Pasco before finally selecting Fancher Field, near East Wenatchee. The jettisoned landing gear required a belly landing, but Pangborn and Herndon were unscathed. The flight took forty-one hours.

Miss Veedol was later sold and disappeared, but her propeller from the Pacific flight is still displayed in the Wenatchee Valley Museum and Cultural Center. Although the flight and Pangborn / Herndon never achieved anything like the fame of Charles Lindbergh and the *Spirit of St. Louis*, the flight is well memorialized in the Wenatchee area. For the serious aviation buff like you and me, this is a trek well worth taking. The Wenatchee area is about a three-hour drive over Highway 2 from Seattle or a short flight that will land you at Pangborn Memorial Airport.

The most historically significant site is the area around old Fancher Field on the heights above East Wenatchee. The airfield closed in the mid-1980s and is now a housing development called Fancher Heights. A tasteful monument to Pangborn-Herndon occupies a prominent spot in this neighborhood overlooking the Columbia River and Wenatchee.

Pangborn-Herndon Memorial
2326 Grand Ave.
East Wenatchee, WA

The Fancher Field location and *Miss Veedol* landing site were a few hundred feet to the northeast of this monument, extending roughly from the corner of Badger Mountain Road and Fancher Blvd. to the corner of Fancher Field Road and Veedol Drive.[2] A surviving hangar structure now sports an attractive mural of Pangborn / Herndon and *Miss Veedol*. Paris - Le Bourget Airport this is not, but the sense of history here is still palpable.

Back down in East Wenatchee, a small but charming park also commemorates the town's most famous visitor. This park includes a *Miss Veedol* weathervane and a small plaque.

Ballard Park
Intersection of Valley Mall Parkway and Hwy 38 (Sunset Hwy)
East Wenatchee, WA

The "Spirit of Wenatchee" project has lovingly created a replica of *Miss Veedol* based at Pangborn Airport. You may see it in the air above the area or on the ramp at the airport.

Spirit of Wenatchee
1 Pangborn Drive
East Wenatchee WA 98802
www.spiritofwenatchee.org

While at Pangborn Airport you might visit Century Aviation, a world class aircraft restoration company.

Century Aviation
3908 Airport Way
East Wenatchee, WA 98802
509-884-0332
www.century-aviation.com

ABOVE

Miss Veedol being prepared for takeoff on a special launch ramp at Sabishiro beach, near Misawa, Japan. The child wears traditional attire to celebrate the occasion. (*Wenatchee Valley Museum & Cultural Center, #80-87-2*)

BELOW

Pangborn and Herndon guide *Miss Veedol* to touchdown at Fancher Field, East Wenatchee, on October 5, 1931. Note the lack of landing gear, which were jettisoned early in the flight to reduce drag and weight. (*Wenatchee Valley Museum & Cultural Center, #80-56-252*)

Monument to Pangborn and Herndon on the heights overlooking East Wenatchee. This location is near the site of Fancher Field, where *Miss Veedol* completed her flight from Japan. (*Author*)

ABOVE

The Spirit of Wenatchee project *Miss Veedol* replica flies over Wenatchee in 2012. (*Author*)

BELOW

Plaque on the Pangborn-Herndon Memorial. (*Author*)

Miss Veedol at rest at Fancher Field, at the end of her epic trans-Pacific flight on October 5, 1931. Note the image is autographed by Pangborn and Herndon. (*Wenatchee Valley Museum & Cultural Center, #80-56-260*)

ABOVE

The approximate site of Fancher Field and *Miss Veedol*'s landing, shown in 2010 with the same Cascade foothills in the distance. (*Author*)

BELOW

The old site of Fancher Field is a housing development now, but this crossroads provides a hint of its history. (*Author*)

East Wenatchee remembers its claim to fame. Ballard Park, near the Columbia River, also celebrates the achievement of Pangborn and Herndon. (*Author*)

PEARSON FIELD, VANCOUVER, WA

Pearson Field in Vancouver—the former site of Vancouver Barracks—is the oldest operating airfield in the US, with ties to dirigible flights in 1905. It was the landing site of a disproportionate number of historically significant flights.

In 1905, young aviator Lincoln Beachey flew his dirigible *Gelatine* daily at the Lewis & Clark Centennial Exposition in Portland. On September 19, he piloted his Baldwin airship northward and forty minutes later arrived at the Vancouver Barracks. This flight was the first air crossing of the Columbia River, the first manned and controlled flight in Washington state, and (since Beachey was carrying a letter to the commandant) the first airmail flight of sorts. Beachey's attempted return flight was frustrated by high winds, but he remained aloft for two hours (a new duration record) before putting down near Orchards, Washington.[3]

Another famous Portland departure ended at what would later become Pearson Field. On June 11, 1912, Silas Christofferson flew a Curtiss pusher biplane off the roof of the Multnomah Hotel in downtown Portland and landed twelve minutes later at the Vancouver Barracks. We'll explore that event and site in the Portland section.

In 1924, the Army Air Service Douglas World Cruiser team transited the air field on their way to Seattle to embark on the first ever air circumnavigation of the globe.

Pearson Field was named for Alexander Pearson (1895–1924), a record-setting army test pilot; he perished in a test accident and the field was named after him in 1925.[4]

It was two unexpected landings of Soviet polar flights in the 1920s and 1930s for which Pearson Field is perhaps best known. On October 18, 1929, the Tupolev ANT-4 *Land of Soviets* diverted to Pearson following trouble with one of its two engines. (The aircraft had made a scheduled stop at Sand Point in Seattle the day before.) After repairs it continued on to San Francisco and its ultimate destination, New York.[5]

On June 20, 1937, another strange Tupolev design, the red-winged ANT-25 *Stalin's Route*, landed at Pearson on its way from Moscow to San Francisco; it too was a victim of engine trouble. Its crew of three, headed by Valery Chkalov, were hailed as heroes and treated to dinner at barracks base commander Gen. George C. Marshall's home.[6]

In modern times, the Pearson Air Museum and Pearson Field Education Center preserve the history of this important airport.

1115 E 5th St. (Museum)
201 East Reserve Street (Education Center)
Vancouver, WA 98661
(360) 816-6232
http://www.nps.gov/fova/historyculture/pearson.htm
http://fortvan.org/Education/Aviation.html

A monument to the Soviet flyers stands on the airfield just a few yards from the Pearson Air Museum hangars.

OPPOSITE

Lincoln Beachey flies his dirigible *Gelatine* over the Oregonian building in downtown Portland during the summer of 1905. The building was demolished in 1950 and stood at 135 S.W. Sixth Ave. Beachey's flight from Portland to the Vancouver Barracks (later Pearson Field) set several significant firsts. (*Oregon Historical Society, ba018567*)

RIGHT

Modern view of Pearson Field, the old hangar, and the Soviet trans-polar flight monument. (*Author*)

BELOW

Tupolev ANT-4 *Land of Soviets* at Pearson Field, October 1929. (*Courtesy of Fort Vancouver National Trust*)

LEFT

Another Soviet trans-polar Tupolev (ANT-25) landed at Pearson Field in June 1937. Its crew is immortalized in the postcard shown here. The phonetic spelling of Cyrillic names varies greatly. (*Courtesy of Fort Vancouver National Trust*)

BELOW LEFT

The ANT-25 at Pearson Field in June 1937. The Pearson hangars still stand today and are part of the Pearson Air Museum and Education Center. (*Courtesy of Fort Vancouver National Trust*)

BELOW

The tremendous wingspan of the long range ANT-25 is apparent in this frontal view at Pearson Field. (*Courtesy of Fort Vancouver National Trust*)

PORTLAND, OR

A wonderful rite of late spring in the "Rose City" is the Rose Festival. The 1912 edition of the celebration featured something extra special: an airplane flight from a downtown rooftop. On June 11, 1912, thousands of on-lookers watched early stunt pilot Silas Christofferson fly a Curtiss pusher biplane off the roof of the Multnomah Hotel in downtown Portland; a custom-built platform was installed on the roof for the event. The flight was a smashing (maybe not the best aviation term) success and also became the first airplane crossing of the Columbia River. Christofferson landed twelve minutes later at the Vancouver Barracks, which would later become Pearson Field.[7]

The Multnomah Hotel building still stands in downtown Portland. After decades of grim duty as a government office building, it was restored to its former glory in the mid-1990s, reopening as the Embassy Suites Downtown in 1997.

Embassy Suites Downtown
319 SW Pine St.
Portland, OR 97204
(503) 279-9000

A small plaque on the 4th Ave. side honors the building's origins as the Multnomah Hotel. Be sure to visit famous Voodoo Doughnuts nearby while you are here!

ABOVE

Silas Christofferson launches from the Multnomah Hotel roof. The special ramp installed for the occasion and large audience are visible. (*Oregon Historical Society, bb008387*)

BELOW

The same building in 2014, the Embassy Suites Downtown. (*Author*)

BOEING 307 CRASH SITE NEAR ALDER, WA

The Boeing 307 Stratoliner was the world's first pressurized airliner, sharing wing and tail structures with the B-17 Flying Fortress bomber. On March 18, 1939, a Boeing demo flight for representatives of KLM and TWA airlines ran into trouble when both engines on one side were shut down to demonstrate controllability. Airspeed was allowed to get too low, the airplane stalled, and it broke up during attempted recovery. The airplane came down near the town of Alder, Washington. All ten occupants on board, including Boeing Chief Engineer Jack Kylstra and KLM pilot Albert von Baumhauer, were killed.[8]

The old town of Alder is now submerged under the artificial lake that formed behind Alder Dam, completed in 1945. The town was located south of today's Sunny Beach Point off WA Highway 7. Remnants of the old Alder can sometimes be seen in late summer when low water levels on Alder Lake reveal the old foundations.[9] The 307 came down just north of Cemetery Road as it runs along the north arm of today's Alder Lake. The main crash site now appears to be submerged.

> **Boeing 307 Crash Site**
> Alder Lake
> Near Cemetery Rd.
> Alder, WA

Wreckage of the 307 Stratoliner near the old town of Alder, WA. Since the airplane broke up in flight debris fell over a wide area. (*The Boeing Company Collection at The Museum of Flight*)

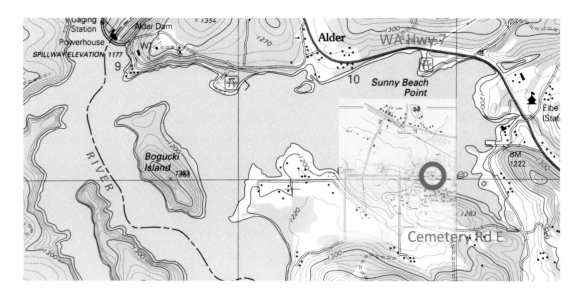

ABOVE

The location of the 1939 307 crash site is shown in this composite of a contemporary accident investigation diagram and a modern topographic map of the north Alder Lake area. The fuselage location is circled, with other debris falling in an area immediately south. The previous route of WA Highway 7 through the old town, now submerged, can be seen. Alder was relocated to its current position on the north edge of the lake when the nearby dam (upper left) was completed in 1945. (*Diagram courtesy of The Boeing Company Collection at The Museum of Flight, map via US Geological Survey (Eatonville, WA 1998)*. A 1937 USGS map of the Eatonville, WA, area was used to correlate the overlay.)

RIGHT

The approximate location of the main crash site lies beyond the exposed stumps in this photo looking northeast from Cemetery Rd. in the autumn of 2014. Sunny Beach Point and the submerged site of old Alder lie across the water out of view to the left of the image. Mt. Rainier looms in the distance. (*Author*)

BOEING 707 CRASH SITE NEAR OSO, WA

A training flight gone wrong ended in the crash of this Boeing 707 in the North Fork of the Stillaguamish River on October 19, 1959. Of a joint Boeing / Braniff crew of eight, four were killed and four escaped with serious injuries. The Civil Aeronautics Board report[10] summarized the events:

> The instructor-pilot initiated a Dutch Roll in which the roll-park [sic] angle of the aircraft reached 40 to 60 degrees. This bank angle is in excess of limitation set by the company for demonstration of [t]his maneuver. The pilot-trainee, who was to make the recovery, rolled full right aileron control while the right rank [sic] was still increasing. The instructor-pilot immediately rolled in full opposite aileron. The airplane stopped its right roll at a point well past a vertical bank and then rolled to the left even more violently. Several gyrations followed and after control of the aircraft was regained, it was determined that three of the four engines had separated from the aircraft and it was on fire. The fire rapidly reduced controllability of the aircraft and an emergency landing was attempted, however, the aircraft struck trees and crashed short of the intended landing area because power on the engine remaining had to be shut down to keep the aircraft wings level.

Interviews with surviving crew members provide further details.[11]

The aircraft came to rest in a bend of the Stillaguamish River very close to Washington Highway 530 at milepost 32, about one mile west of the town of Oso. (Oso would experience another tragedy on March 22, 2014, when a mudslide took the lives of forty-three people.)

Unfortunately, there is no public access to the river near the accident site. Please don't trespass.

Boeing 707 Crash Site
WA State Highway 530
Milepost 32
Near Oso, WA

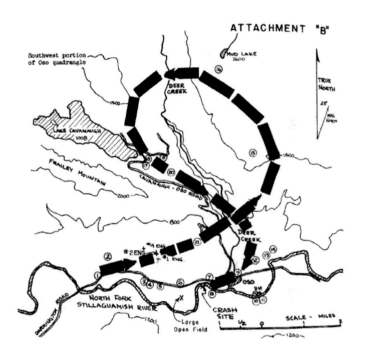

CIRCLED NUMBERS INDICATE
LOCATION OF EYE WITNESSES.

Diagram from the Civil Aeronautics Board Aircraft Accident Report on Boeing 707 N7071 showing the ground track in the final moments of the flight near Oso, WA. Washington Highway 530, labeled "Darrington Road," snakes along the bottom of the map alongside the North Fork of the Stillaguamish River. (*US Civil Aeronautics Board*)

ABOVE

The stricken 707 flew over Deer Creek here just before impact in the North Fork of the Stillaguamish River a few hundred yards to the right (west) of this image. (*Author*)

BELOW

The airplane came to rest in the river about 100 yards over the edge of this meadow near milepost 32 on WA Highway 530. (*Author*)

OTHER HISTORIC AIRFIELDS

We've already visited several historic airports in the Northwest, but there are many more. We'll explore a few of them here...

Bellevue Airfield, Bellevue, WA

A vibrant general aviation airport once existed in the Eastgate area of Bellevue. It was closed in 1982 and is now occupied primarily by Boeing and Microsoft office buildings and the Embassy Suites Seattle-Bellevue at 3225 158th Ave. SE.[12]

Issaquah Skyport, Issaquah, WA

The Seattle area hub for skydiving was once located at this airport, which closed in 1987. It is now the location of a shopping complex south of NW Sammamish Rd at 11th Ave. NW.[13]

Arlington Municipal Airport (AWO), Arlington, WA

This airport is very much alive and well, and is famous as the home of the Arlington Fly-In in early July of each year. The airfield was established in 1934. Today it hosts multiple aviation manufacturing enterprises as well as general aviation.

Arlington Airport
18204 59th Dr. NE
Arlington, WA 98223
www.arlingtonflyin.org

Naval Air Station Whidbey Island (NUW), Oak Harbor, WA

The US Navy's premier air facility in the Northwest became active in September 1942. Its original purpose was a base to support PBY Catalina flying boats, but an airfield (Ault Field) was also constructed that would have a larger long term role.[14] (Commander William Ault was lost during the World War II Battle of the Coral Sea.) Wildcat and Hellcat pilots trained here during World War II. In later years the base became the home of the navy's electronic attack squadrons, flying such aircraft as the EA-6B Prowler and F/A-18G Growler, as well as P-3 Orion maritime patrol aircraft. The base typically has an annual public open house in the summer, with the latest information at the website http://cnic.navy.mil/regions/cnrnw/installations/nas_whidbey_island.html.

About ten miles south of NAS Whidbey is Naval Outlying Field Coupeville. This small airstrip emulates an aircraft carrier on dry land that is used by Prowler and Growler aviators over the years to maintain carrier landing proficiency. You can observe the action from Washington Highway 20, which skirts the facility about three miles east of Coupeville. Be prepared for loud noise!

Boeing XB-47 Stratojet conducting the first Jet Assisted Takeoff (JATO) test from Moses Lake, WA, circa 1950. The extra thrust from a cluster of small rockets installed on both sides of the fuselage significantly improved takeoff performance. This spectacular sight would be repeated many times in US Air Force service. (*Copyright © Boeing – used with permission*)

Grant County Airport (MWH), Moses Lake WA
Larson Air Force Base was established for training during World War II, and its runways were greatly expanded to support postwar B-47s and B-52s of the Strategic Air Command. The first flights of the XB-47 and YB-52 landed here. The base closed in 1966 and it has operated as a civil airport ever since.[15] Aside from general aviation and some cargo operations, the airport's long runways and favorable weather have made it a popular location for Boeing flight test activities. Japan Airlines maintained a 747 training facility here from 1968 to 2009. Of particular note is Runway 14L/32R, which is 13,500 feet long.[16]

Grant County Airport
7810 Andrews St. NE #200
Moses Lake, WA 98837

Felts Field (SFF), Spokane, WA
Just east of downtown, alongside the Spokane River, lies this airport with aviation roots as far back as 1913. Known originally as Parkwater Airstrip, it was renamed for James Felts—another in a long line of fallen aviators—in 1927. That September, it was visited by Charles Lindbergh on his good will tour and hosted the National Air Races. It was the aviation hub of the city until commercial activity moved to Geiger Field (west of the city) after World War II.[17] It was also the home base for the August 1929 120-hour endurance flight by Nick Mamer and Art Walker in the Buhl CA-6 christened *Spokane Sun-God*.[18] Today it remains an active general aviation airport.

Felts Field
6105 E Rutter Ave.
Spokane, WA

A Northwest Airlines DC-3 in transit at Felts Field, Spokane, WA, in the late 1930s. Northwest began serving Spokane in 1934. The terminal building still stands and includes the landmark Skyway Café. (*Northwest Museum of Arts & Culture*)

Fairchild Air Force Base (SKA), Spokane, WA

Beginning as Spokane Army Airfield in 1942 and named for General Muir Fairchild in 1950, this base on the west side of the city has been the continuous home of KC-135 Stratotankers since 1958. The aerial refueling mission has been the common thread here, but the base has also hosted B-29s, B-36 Peacemakers, and was a longtime home for the B-52s of the 92nd Bombardment Wing. Several Atlas intercontinental ballistic missile sites were installed in the area and controlled from Fairchild in the early 1960s. Monthly base tours are conducted during the summer months—check the following website for current information: http://www.fairchild.af.mil/units/publicaffairs/communityrelations/basetours.asp.

Rogue Valley International—Medford Airport, Medford, OR

Formerly known as the Medford-Jackson County Airport, this facility has the distinction of being the first municipal airport in Oregon. The first significant tenant was Vern Gorst's Pacific Air Transport Company, part of his burgeoning West Coast air mail business in the late 1920s. Major upgrades to runway, lighting, radio, and weather capabilities in 1930 enabled the growth of passenger service during the following decade.[19] Civil operations continued during World War II. In August 1944, in a far-sighted demonstration of postwar opportunity, a United Airlines DC-3 flew a full load of fruit, flowers, and fish from Medford to New York City—the first coast-to-coast flight of perishable cargo.[20] The airport gained notoriety in the 1960s as a fire base for numerous air tankers. Modified B-17s, DC-6s, PB4Y Privateers, and other types were a common site during this period and fire bombers continue to operate here to the present day. In the twenty-first century, a modernized Medford airport is served by multiple airlines. It occupies the same location as the original airfield, but all of the original structures are gone.

Medford Airport
1000 Terminal Spur Rd.
Medford, OR 97504

Still Others…

We have neglected many other historic fields worthy of your attention: Geiger Field in Spokane, Pasco Airport (now Tri-Cities Airport), Yakima Air Terminal / McAllister Field, Portland International Airport, and dozens of small local fields. The list goes on, and interested readers are encouraged to research and discover these places that have left their mark on aviation in the Pacific Northwest.

BELOW

Pacific Air Transport Ryan M-1 mail plane at Medford, Oregon, in the late 1920s. The airplane sports the name *Medford* on its nose. (*The Museum of Flight Collection*)

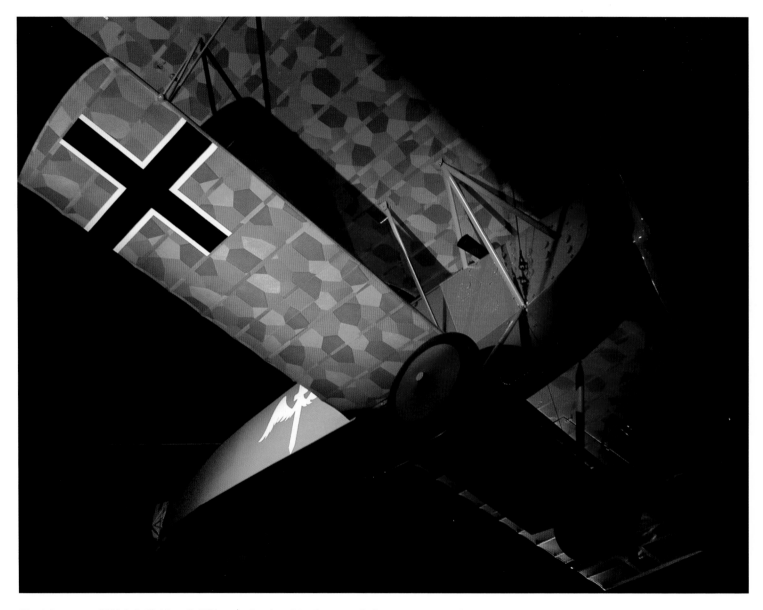

The Museum of Flight's Fokker D.VII reproduction. Northwest aviation museums and flying collections cover everything an enthusiast might dream to see. (*Author*)

CHAPTER NINE

NORTHWEST AVIATION MUSEUMS

We've been able to visit several top notch museums in our journey thus far. In this section, we provide a thorough list of most flight-related museums in the region. (Note: the museum business is unfortunately not always stable, so do check before you embark on a visit.)

NORTHWEST AIR MUSEUMS—WASHINGTON

Flying Heritage Collection
- see page 130

Future of Flight
(Aviation Center & Boeing Everett Tour)
- see page 130

Heritage Flight Museum
15053 Crosswind Dr.
Burlington, WA 98233
(360) 424-5151
www.heritageflight.org

Historic Flight Foundation
- see page 130

Legend Flyers
(Me-262 Project)
- see page 130

McAllister Museum of Aviation
2008 S 16th Avenue
Yakima, WA 98903
(509) 457-4933
www.mcallistermuseum.org

McChord Air Museum
- see page 108

The Museum of Flight
- see page 15

The Museum of Flight Restoration Center and Reserve Collection
- see page 130

North Cascades Vintage Aircraft Museum
7879 South Superior Avenue #6
Concrete, WA 98237
(360) 770-4848
www.vintageaircraftmuseum.org

Olympic Flight Museum
7637-A Old Highway 99 SE
Olympia, WA 98501
(360) 705-3925
www.olympicflightmuseum.org

PBY - Naval Air Museum
270 SE Pioneer Way
Oak Harbor, WA 98277
(360) 240-9500
http://pbymf.org/

Pearson Air Museum
- see page 138

Port Townsend Aero Museum
105 Airport Road
Jefferson County International Airport
Port Townsend, WA 98368
(360) 379-5244
www.ptaeromuseum.com

NORTHWEST AIR MUSEUMS—OREGON

Erickson Aircraft Collection
2408 NW Berg Drive
Madras, OR, 97741
(541) 460-5065
www.ericksoncollection.com

Evergreen Aviation & Space Museum
500 NE Capt Michael King Smith Way
McMinnville, OR
(503) 434-4180
www.evergreenmuseum.org

Oregon Air & Space Museum
90377 Boeing Drive
Eugene, OR 97402
(541) 461-1101
www.oasm.info

Tillamook Air Museum
6030 Hangar Rd.
Tillamook, OR
(503) 842-1130
www.tillamookair.com

Western Antique Aeroplane & Automobile Museum
1600 Air Museum Rd.
Hood River, OR
(541) 308-1600
www.waaamuseum.org

NORTHWEST AIR MUSEUMS—BRITISH COLUMBIA, CANADA

British Columbia Aviation Museum
1910 Norseman Road
Sidney, BC
Canada, V8L 5V5
(250) 655-3300
www.bcam.net

Canadian Museum of Flight
Hangar # 3 - 5333 216th Street
Langley, BC V2Y 2N3
(604) 532-0035
www.canadianflight.org

Eighty years of Seattle aviation fly in formation. The first Boeing 787 Dreamliner flies with the Model 40C restoration owned and flown by Addison Pemberton. This Model 40 (serial number 1043) is the oldest flying Boeing aircraft.
(*Copyright © Boeing – used with permission*)

CHAPTER 1 ENDNOTES

1. David Wilma, "Meadows Race Track," *HistoryLing.org Essay 2995*, February 19, 2001. http://www.historylink.org/index.cfm?displaypage=output.cfm&file_id=2995

2. Carroll Gray, Emails to the author and Dan Hagedorn, July 22–23, 2009.

3. Alan J. Stein, "Charles Hamilton pilots the first airplane in Washington on March 11, 1910," *HistoryLink.org Essay 5423,* April 9, 2013, http://www.historylink.org/index.cfm?DisplayPage=output.cfm&file_id=5423

4. Paul Spitzer, "Showman: C.K. Hamilton, the Flying Daredevil," *Columbia*, 1994 Vol. 8 No. 1

5. Spitzer, "Showman"

6. Wilma, "Meadows Race Track"

7. Dan Hagedorn, ed., *The Museum of Flight, A Collected History*, (Seattle, WA: Sea Script Company, 2012), 10–26

8. Cory Graff, *Boeing Field*, (Charleston, SC: Arcadia Publishing, 2008), 7–8.

9. Harold Mansfield, *Vision*, (New York, NY: Madison Publishing Associates, 2nd ed., 1986), 211.

10. Ibid, 94, 99, 105, 120, 141, 151, 204, 283, 338; Mike Lombardi, notes to author, December 2014; Larry Davis, *P-26 Mini in Action*, (Carrollton, TX: Squadron/

Signal Publications, 1994), 4; and Nicholas A. Veronico, *Boeing 377 Stratocruiser*, (North Branch, MN: Specialty Press, 2002), 18.

11. Daryl C. McClary, "U.S. Air Force B-52 on a low-level test flight crashes near Burns, Oregon, killing five Boeing employees, on June 23, 1959," HistoryLink.org Essay 10063, April 2, 2012. http://www.historylink.org/index.cfm?DisplayPage=output.cfm&file_id=10063.

12. Terry Stephens, "Vern Gorst," Accessed September 15, 2014. http://julyjubilee.com/2012/06/vern-gorst-site-dedication/

13. Ed Davies and Steve Ellis, *Seattle's Commercial Aviation, 1910-1941*, (Charleston, SC: Arcadia Publishing, 2009), 35–40.

14. Peter M. Bowers, *Boeing Since 1916*. (Annapolis, MD: Naval Institute Press (USA), 1988), 34–35.

15. Ibid; Boeing Historical Archives, *Year by Year: 75 Years of Boeing History 1916-1991*, (Seattle, WA: Boeing Historical Archives, 1991), 3, 6, 12, 39, 40; Mansfield, 28, 34, 93, 137; Peter M. Bowers, *Flying the Boeing Model 80.* (Seattle, WA: Museum of Flight, 1984), 12; Mike Lombardi, notes to author, December 2014.

16. Mansfield, 86.

17. Ibid. 280, 281, 342; Boeing Historical Archives, *Year by Year*, 39, 40, 77; Bowers, *Boeing*, 494; 737 Commercial Transport, Historical Snapshot, Accessed April 26, 2015. http://www.boeing.com/history/products/737-classic.page; Mike Lombardi, notes to author, December 2014.
18. Mike Lombardi, "50 Years at the Leading Edge," *Boeing Frontiers*, August 2009. http://www.boeing.com/news/frontiers/archive/2009/august/i_history.pdf; Boeing Historical Archives, *Year by Year*, 86, 119; Bowers, *Boeing*, 554.
19. Dominic Gates, "New Life at Boeing for an Old Factory Floor." *The Seattle Times*, June 8, 2011.
20. Boeing Historical Archives, *Year by Year*, 52.
21. Ibid. 51.
22. Alan J. Stein, "B-50 Bomber crashes into the Lester Apartments near Boeing Field, killing 11, on August 13, 1951," *HistoryLink.org Essay 3969*. October 2, 2002. http://www.historylink.org/index.cfm?DisplayPage=output.cfm&File_Id=3969

CHAPTER 2 ENDNOTES

1. Paul G. Spitzer, "The Aero Club of the Northwest, 1915-1920," *Eastlake News*, November/December 2007
2. Bowers, *Boeing*, 34–35.
3. Mansfield, 14–17, 34; Boeing Historical Archives, *Year by Year*, 2–3.
4. Mansfield, 32.
5. Davies and Ellis, 70–71.

CHAPTER 3 ENDNOTES

1. Aaron J. Naff, *Seattle's Luna Park*. (Charleston, SC: Arcadia Publishing, 2011), 75–86.
2. M.D. Klaas, *Last of the Flying Clippers, The Boeing 314 Story*, (Atglen, PA: Schiffer Publishing Ltd., 1997), 78–81.
3. Davies and Ellis, 13.
4. Ibid. 68–69.
5. Mansfield, 47.
6. "The Hoge Building," Accessed April 28, 2015. http://www.nps.gov/nr/travel/seattle/s24.htm
7. Paula Becker, et al., *The Future Remembered: The 1962 Seattle World's Fair and Its Legacy*, (Seattle, WA: Seattle Center Foundation, 2011), 104–106, 155–156, 188, 252.

CHAPTER 4 ENDNOTES

1. Alan J. Stein, et al., *Alaska-Yukon-Pacific Exposition*,(Seattle, WA: History Ink, 2009), 23.
2. Ibid. 49, 52, 57, 59, 71.

3. J. Lee, et al., *A History of the University of Washington Department of Aeronautics and Astronautics 1917-2003*, May 27, 2003, https://www.uwal.org/uwalinfo/AA_History.pdf.
4. Northwest Maritime Heritage, "University Shell House," Accessed June 21, 2015. http://threesheetsnw.com/maritimeheritage/attractions/university-shell-house/
5. Carroll V. Glines, *The First Flight Around the World*, (Missoula, MT: Pictorial Histories Publishing Co., 2000), 19–21, 40, 57, 137.
6. Davies and Ellis, 41.
7. Ibid. 112.
8. Boeing Historical Archives, *Year by Year*, 76–78.
9. A. M. "Tex" Johnston, *Tex Johnston: Jet Age Test Pilot*, (Washington, D.C.: Smithsonian Books, 1991), 202–203.
10. Rebecca Wallick, *Growing Up Boeing: The Early Jet Age Through the Eyes of a Test Pilot's Daughter*, (Lynnwood, WA: Maian Meadows Publishing, 2014), 50.
11. Kenmore Air, www.kenmoreair.com
12. Duane Colt Denfield, Ph.D., "Nike Missile Bases: Washington Cold War Defenses," *HistoryLink.org Essay 9711*. March 19, 2011. http://www.historylink.org/index.cfm?DisplayPage=output.cfm&file_id=9711; Ed Thelen, *Nike Missile Sites, Washington*, http://ed-thelen.org/loc-w.html#Washington.

CHAPTER 5 ENDNOTES

1. Walt Crowley, "Sea-Tac International Airport: Part 1—Founding," *HistoryLink.org Essay 1004*, April 2, 1999. http://www.historylink.org/index.cfm?DisplayPage=output.cfm&file_id=1004
2. Walt Crowley, "Sea-Tac International Airport: Part 2—From Props to Jets (1950-1970)," *HistoryLink.org Essay 4232*, August 17, 2003. http://www.historylink.org/index.cfm?DisplayPage=output.cfm&file_id=4232
3. Ibid.
4. Walt Crowley, "Sea-Tac International Airport: Part 3—Boeing Bust to Deregulation (1970s)," *HistoryLink.org Essay 4233*, August 17, 2003. http://www.historylink.org/index.cfm?DisplayPage=output.cfm&file_id=4233
5. Bowers, *Boeing*, 53.
6. Paul Freeman, "Abandoned & Little-Known Airfields: Washington, Seattle Area," accessed April 30, 2015. http://www.airfields-freeman.com/WA/Airfields_WA_Seattle.htm#kent1st; Davies and Ellis, 65.
7. Paul Freeman, "Abandoned & Little-Known Airfields: Washington, Seattle Area," accessed April 30, 2015. http://www.airfields-freeman.com/WA/Airfields_WA_Seattle.htm#kent2nd.
8. CAB Accident Report, SA-159, File No. 1-0094. May 20, 1949. http://specialcollection.dotlibrary.dot.gov/Document?db=DOT-AIRPLANEACCIDENTS&query=(select+364).

9. CAB Accident Report, SA-319, File No. 1-0051. November 14, 1956. http://specialcollection.dotlibrary.dot.gov/Document?db=DOT-AIRPLANEACCIDENTS&query=(select+623)

10. Bruce Haulman, "The Other Maury Island Incident," http://vashonhistory.com/Publications/time_and_again/other_maury_island_incident.pdf

11. Boeing Historical Archives, *Year by Year*, 117, 130; John Caldbick, "The Boeing Company wins NASA contract for lunar rover on October 28, 1969," *HistoryLink.org Essay 10045*, February 28, 2012. http://www.historylink.org/index.cfm?displaypage=output.cfm&file_id=10045; Steve Wilhelm, "Boeing Space Center in Kent gave birth to coolest technology of the day," *Puget Sound Business Journal*, December 12, 2012. http://www.bizjournals.com/seattle/news/2012/12/12/boeing-once-built-slick-vehicles-at.html

12. Paul Freeman, "Abandoned & Little-Known Airfields: Washington, Seattle Area," Accessed May 3, 2015. http://www.airfields-freeman.com/WA/Airfields_WA_Tacoma.htm#cloverpark

13. Kimberly Peterson, *McChord Field*, (Charleston, CA: Arcadia Publishing, 2013), 7; Duane Colt Denfeld, "McChord Field, McChord Air Force Base, and Joint Base Lewis-McChord: Part 1," *HistoryLink.org Essay 9934*, October 25, 2011. http://www.historylink.org/index.cfm?DisplayPage=output.cfm&file_id=9934

14. Peterson, 8.

15. Duane Colt Denfeld, "Fort Lewis: Gray Army Airfield," *HistoryLink.org Essay 8623*, June 16, 2008. http://www.historylink.org/index.cfm?DisplayPage=output.cfm&file_id=8623

CHAPTER 6 ENDNOTES

1. Eleanor Boba, "Point of No Return: The Will Rogers-Wiley Post Memorial Seaplane Base (Renton)," *HistoryLink.org Essay 10972*, November 17, 2014. http://www.historylink.org/index.cfm?DisplayPage=output.cfm&file_id=10972

2. Boeing Historical Archives, *Year by Year*, 47.

3. Mansfield, 344; Robert Redding and Bill Yenne, *Boeing, Planemaker to the World*, (Greenwich, CT: Bison Books Corp., 1983), 173, 242.

CHAPTER 7 ENDNOTES

1. Bertrand, Steve K., *Paine Field*, (Charleston, SC: Arcadia Publishing, 2014), 7.

2. Ibid. 34.

3. Ibid. 97–106.

4. Redding and Yenne, 193; Guy Norris and Mark Wagner, *Boeing*, (Osceola, WI: MBI Publishing, 1998), 161–162; Karl Sabbagh, *Twenty-First-Century Jet, The Making and Marketing of the Boeing 777*, (New York, NY: Scribner, 1996), 275–277; Lori Gunter, "Dream Flight," *Boeing Frontiers*, February 2010. http://www.boeing.com/news/frontiers/archive/2010/february/cover.pdf

CHAPTER 8 ENDNOTES

1. David Nevin, *The Epic of Flight: The Pathfinders*. (Alexandria, VA: Time-Life Books, 1980), 144–145.

2. Paul Freeman, "Abandoned & Little-Known Airfields: Central Washington State," Accessed April 30, 2015. http://www.airfields-freeman.com/WA/Airfields_WA_C.htm#fancher

3. Bill Alley, *Pearson Field*, (Charleston, SC: Arcadia Publishing, 2006), 11–13.

4. Ibid. 39.

5. Ibid. 67–69.

6. Ibid. 70–78.

7. Ibid. 20–22.

8. Mansfield, 158; Robert J. Serling, *Legend and Legacy: The Story of Boeing and Its People*, (New York, NY: St. Martin's Press, 1992), 44–46.

9. Tim Nyhus, *Ghost Towns of Washington, Alder*, Accessed October 10, 2014. http://www.ghosttownsofwashington.com/alder.html

10. CAB Accident Report, SA-347, File No. 2-1754, June 20, 1960. http://specialcollection.dotlibrary.dot.gov/Document?db=DOT-AIRPLANEACCIDENTS&query=(select+682)

11. Rebecca Wallick, *Growing Up Boeing: The Early Jet Age Through the Eyes of a Test Pilot's Daughter*, (Lynnwood, WA: Maian Meadows Publishing, 2014), 104–118.

12. Paul Freeman, "Abandoned & Little-Known Airfields: Washington, Seattle Area," Accessed May 3, 2015. http://www.airfields-freeman.com/WA/Airfields_WA_Seattle.htm#bellevue

13. Paul Freeman, "Abandoned & Little-Known Airfields: Washington, Seattle Area," Accessed May 3, 2015. http://www.airfields-freeman.com/WA/Airfields_WA_Seattle.htm#issaquah

14. David Wilma, "Naval Air Station Whidbey Island is formally commissioned on September 21, 1942," HistoryLink.org Essay 8228, July 26, 2007. http://www.historylink.org/index.cfm?displaypage=output.cfm&file_id=8228

15. Duane Colt Denfeld, "Larson Air Force Base -- Grant County International Airport," *HistoryLink.org Essay 10147*, August 27, 2012. http://www.historylink.org/index.cfm?DisplayPage=output.cfm&file_id=10147

16. Grant County International Airport, Port of Moses Lake, http://www.portofmoseslake.com/key-industries/aerospace/

17. Laura Arksey, "Felts Field (Spokane)," *HistoryLink.org Essay 8464*, January 15, 2008. http://www.historylink.org/index.cfm?DisplayPage=output.cfm&file_id=8464

18. Richard L. Meister Jr., "The Flight of the Spokane Sun-God," Accessed February 20, 2015. http://www.aerofiles.com/sungod.html

19. Bill Alley and the Southern Oregon Historical Society, *Aviation in Southern Oregon*, (Charleston, SC: Arcadia Publishing, 2011), 7–9.

20. Hattie B. Becker, *The History of the Rogue Valley International-Medford*, (Medford, OR: Jackson County Airport Authority, 1995), 15.

BIBLIOGRAPHY

Allen, Oliver E. *The Epic of Flight: The Airline Builders.* Alexandria, VA: Time-Life Books, 1981.

Alley, Bill and the Southern Oregon Historical Society. *Aviation in Southern Oregon.* Charleston, SC: Arcadia Publishing, 2011.

Alley, Bill. *Pearson Field.* Charleston, SC: Arcadia Publishing, 2006.

Arlington Fly-In, www.arlingtonflyin.org

Bauer, Eugene E. *Boeing: The First Century.* Issaquah, WA: Taba Publishing, 2000.

Becker, Hattie B. *The History of the Rogue Valley International-Medford.* (Medford, OR: Jackson County Airport Authority, 1995.

Becker, Paula, Alan J. Stein, & HistoryLink Staff. *The Future Remembered: The 1962 Seattle World's Fair and Its Legacy.* Seattle, WA: Seattle Center Foundation, 2011.

Bertrand, Steve K. *Paine Field.* Charleston, SC: Arcadia Publishing, 2014.

Birdsall, Steve. *B-29 Superfortress in Action.* Carrollton, TX: Squadron/Signal Publications, 1977.

Boeing Historical Archives. *Year by Year: 75 Years of Boeing History 1916-1991.* Seattle, WA: Boeing Historical Archives, 1991.

Bogash, Robert. *In Search of an Icon: The Hunt for...the Honolulu Clipper*, last modified November 1, 2010, rbogash.com/B314.html.

Bowers, Peter M. *B-17 Flying Fortress.* Seattle, WA: Museum of Flight, 1985.

Bowers, Peter M. *Boeing Since 1916.* Annapolis, MD: Naval Institute Press USA, 1988.

Bowers, Peter M. *Flying the Boeing Model 80.* Seattle, WA: Museum of Flight, 1984.

Brown, James A. *Hubbard: The Forgotten Boeing Aviator.* Seattle, WA: Peanut Butter Publishing, 1996.

Davies, Ed and Steve Ellis. *Seattle's Commercial Aviation, 1910-1941.* Charleston, SC: Arcadia Publishing, 2009.

Davis, Larry. *P-12/F4B in Action.* Carrollton, TX: Squadron/Signal Publications, 1993.

Davis, Larry. *P-26 Mini in Action.* Carrollton, TX: Squadron/Signal Publications, 1994.

Dorpat, Paul. *Seattle Now & Then* 3 Volumes, Seattle, WA: Tartu Publications, 1986-90.

DorpatSherrardLomont, Seattle Now & Then. pauldorpat.com.

Drendl, Lou & Tom Y'Blood. *Boeing B-47 Stratojet in Action.* Carrollton, TX: Squadron/Signal Publications, 1976.

Drendl, Lou. *Boeing B-52 Stratofortress in Action.* Carrollton, TX: Squadron/Signal Publications, 1975.

Faure, C. Marin. *Success on the Step.* Seattle, WA: Elton-Wolf Publishing, 2004

Freeman, Paul F. *Abandoned & Little-Known Airfields: Washington.* http://www.airfields-freeman.com/WA/Airfields_WA.htm.

Glines, Carroll V. *The First Flight Around the World.* Missoula, MT: Pictorial Histories Publishing Co., 2000

Gordon, David. *Wings Over Washington.* Santa Barbara, CA: Sequoia Communications, 1989.

Graff, Cory. *Boeing Field.* Charleston, SC: Arcadia Publishing, 2008.

Hagedorn, Dan, ed. *The Museum of Flight, A Collected History.* Seattle, WA: Sea Script Company, 2012.

Heickell, Edward T. & Robert L. Heickell. *One Chance for Glory: First Nonstop Flight Across the Pacific.* North Charleston, SC: CreateSpace Independent Publishing Platform, 2012.

Historylink.org, *The Online Encyclopedia of Washington State History.* www.historyLink.org

Hollenbeck, Cliff & Nancy, *Alaska Airlines*, Anchorage, AK: Everbest Printing Co. Ltd., 2012.

Irving, Clive. *Wide-Body: The Triumph of the 747.* New York, NY: William Morrow & Company, 1993.

Jackson, Donald Dale. *The Epic of Flight: The Explorers.* Alexandria, VA: Time-Life Books, 1983.

Johnston, A. M. "Tex" *Tex Johnston: Jet Age Test Pilot.* Washington, D.C.: Smithsonian Books, 1991.

156

Kenmore Air, www.kenmoreair.com

Klaas, M.D. *Last of the Flying Clippers, The Boeing 314 Story*, Atglen, PA: Schiffer Publishing Ltd., 1997.

Kroll Map Company. 2700 3rd Ave, Seattle WA 98121, www.krollmap.com

Lavelle, Mike & Addison Pemberton. *The Model 40: The History of the Boeing Model 40 and the Birth of Boeing Airliners*. Chestertown, MD: Chester River Press, 2012.

Lee, J., D.S. Eberhardt, R.E. Breidenthal, & A.P. Bruckner. *A History of the University of Washington Department of Aeronautics and Astronautics 1917-2003*. May 27, 2003, https://www.uwal.org/uwalinfo/AA_History.pdf.

Lloyd, Alwyn T. *B-29 Superfortress in Detail & Scale*. Fallbrook, CA: Aero Publishers, Inc., 1983.

Mansfield, Harold. *Vision*. New York, NY: Madison Publishing Associates, 2nd ed., 1986.

Meister, Richard L. *The Flight of the Spokane Sun-God*. http://www.aerofiles.com/sungod.html.

Naff, Aaron J. *Seattle's Luna Park*. Charleston, SC: Arcadia Publishing, 2011.

Nevin, David. *The Epic of Flight: The Pathfinders*. Alexandria, VA: Time-Life Books, 1980.

Norris, Guy and Mark Wagner. *Boeing*. Osceola, WI: MBI Publishing, 1998

Peterson, Kimberly. *McChord Field*. Charleston, CA: Arcadia Publishing, 2013.

Redding, Robert & Bill Yenne. *Boeing, Planemaker to the World*. Greenwich, CT: Bison Books Corp., 1983

Sabbagh, Karl. *Twenty-First-Century Jet, The Making and Marketing of the Boeing 777*. New York, NY: Scribner, 1996.

The Seattle World Cruiser Project. www.seattleworldcruiser.org.

Serling, Robert J. *Character & Characters, The Spirit of Alaska Airlines*. Seattle, WA: Documentary Media LLC, 2008.

Serling, Robert J. *Legend and Legacy: The Story of Boeing and Its People*. New York, NY: St. Martin's Press, 1992.

Serling, Robert J. *The Epic of Flight: The Jet Age*. Alexandria, VA: Time-Life Books, 1982.

Stein, Alan J., Paula Becker, & HistoryLink Staff. *Alaska-Yukon-Pacific Exposition*. Seattle, WA: History Ink, 2009.

Sterling, Bryan B. & Frances N. Sterling. *Forgotten Eagle: Wiley Post, America's Heroic Aviation Pioneer*. New York, NY: Carroll & Graf Publishers, 2001.

Stoff, Joshua. *Picture History of World War II American Aircraft Production*. New York, NY: Dover Publications, Inc., 1993.

Sutter, Joe with Jay Spenser. *747*. New York, NY: Smithsonian Books with Harper Collins, 2006.

Thelen, Ed. *Nike Missile Sites, Washington*. http://ed-thelen.org/loc-w.html#Washington.

United States Geological Survey, http://www.usgs.gov/pubprod/maps.html.

University of Washington Digital Collections. *When the World Came to Campus, AYPE 1909*. https://content.lib.washington.edu/exhibits/aype/index.html.

Van Der Linden, F. Robert. *The Boeing 247, The First Modern Airliner*. Seattle, WA: University of Washington Press, 1991.

Veronico, Nicholas A. *Boeing 377 Stratocruiser*. North Branch, MN: Specialty Press, 2002.

Wallick, Rebecca. *Growing Up Boeing: The Early Jet Age Through the Eyes of a Test Pilot's Daughter*. Lynnwood, WA: Maian Meadows Publishing, 2014

Wallick, S.L. "Lew" and Peter M. Bowers. *Flying the P-12*. Seattle, WA: Museum of Flight, 1982.

Yenne, Bill. *The American Aircraft Factory in WWII*. Minneapolis, MN: Zenith Press, 2006.

INDEX